LINCOLN CHRISTIAN UNIV

O9-BTO-380

IN GOD'S PRESENCE

IN GOD'S PRESENCE

ENCOUNTERING, EXPERIENCING, AND EMBRACING THE HOLY IN WORSHIP

N. GRAHAM STANDISH

THE
ALBAN
INSTITUTE
Herndon, Virginia
www.alban.org

Copyright © 2010 by The Alban Institute. All rights reserved. This material may not be photocopied or reproduced in any way without written permission. Go to www.alban.org/permissions.asp or write to the address below.

The Alban Institute
2121 Cooperative Way, Suite 100
Herndon, VA 20171

Unless otherwise noted, all Scripture quotations are from the New Revised Standard Version of the Bible, © 1989, Division of Christian Education of the National Council of Churches of Christ in the United States of America, and are used by permission.

Cover design by Tobias Becker, Bird Box Design.

Library of Congress Cataloging-in-Publication Data

Standish, N. Graham, 1959-
  In God's presence : encountering, experiencing, and embracing the holy in worship / N. Graham Standish.
      p. cm.
  Includes bibliographical references.
  ISBN 978-1-56699-405-7
  1. Public worship. 2. God--Worship and love. I. Alban Institute. II. Title.
  BV15.S6915 2010
  264--dc22
                          2010020075

    10   11   12   13   14   VG   5   4   3   2   1

Contents

———•◆•———

122060

To Toni Schlemmer, Bruce Smith, and DeWayne Segafredo:
The three of you have taught me so much about worship,
and much of what I've written are insights
gained from the privilege of working with you.
I appreciate you more than you know.

Introduction

THE WORSHIP SERVICE WAS MEMORABLE FOR A LOT OF REASONS. IT WAS memorable because I had never been to a contemporary service before, but mostly it was memorable because of my wife's reaction to it. My wife was and is Roman Catholic. She'd had even less exposure to contemporary worship than I. Prior to my talking about it, she hadn't even heard of contemporary worship.

So off we went to a nondenominational church in our area to see how they did worship. About halfway through the service, my wife saw that they were planning on doing their version of passing the peace. As they were getting ready, she leaned over to me and whispered, "Can we leave?" I said, "Why? We're not even halfway through." She replied, "I'm worried about them shaking my hand. I don't want to have some sort of conversion experience. I have things to do today." I burst out laughing and had to contain myself to keep from disrupting the service.

The service itself was a run-of-the-mill evangelical contemporary service, yet it included something I had never witnessed before. The pastor talked about how Christ was calling us to experience him and to feel his presence in our lives. He then said, "If any of you visiting today have not had an experience like this, there are conversion counselors in the lobby who are glad to talk with you about Christ and how you can experience him in your life." I was curious. What does a conversion counselor say? I'm sure I made some smart-aleck comment to my wife that she could visit the conversion counselor to help her get over her fears of passing the peace.

I have not been a fan of contemporary services, including the one at that church. It had a lot of energy, but it seemed to lack depth and substance. I felt like I was being given a long sales pitch from the moment I walked in. The fact that we were invited to see a conversion counselor made it seem even more like a sales pitch. They very easily could have said that we could visit one of their conversion salesclerks, and the suggestion would have felt the same way. As a counselor myself, with a master's degree in counseling and training as a spiritual director as part of my doctorate in spiritual formation, I kept wondering what kind of training a conversion counselor would get. Did it include field placement? Did it include any classroom hours? Could people receive third-party payments as conversion counselors? Still, I was fascinated by this congregation's worship because it was so different from what I grew up experiencing.

The period of my life when I visited that church was a great time for me, because I was learning how many different forms of worship there are. From an early age I had felt uncomfortable with traditional Christian worship. I was not a happy churchgoer as a child and teen. I learned to detest the organ except when played by rock bands such as the Allman Brothers, Sugarloaf, or other bands from the 1960s and '70s. I also hated the pace of traditional worship. I also didn't care much for the preaching, because it never seemed to touch the things I was concerned with. The worship services I grew up with seemed so *slooooooooooooooow*. At times in church, the combination of the music, the pace, and the atmosphere caused me to twitch, twitter, and fidget like I had gibbons in my gutchies. When I became a pastor in 1988, I was resigned to the fact that for the rest of my life I would be leading worship that I generally didn't like and that barely inspired me.

The first church I served as an associate pastor was a typically traditional Presbyterian church. I believe that the senior pastor and I—through our preaching, children's sermons, and ways of praying—injected life into the congregation, but the music was much the same as it had been when I grew up. In fact, I remember the music director once saying within my earshot that no sacred music composed after 1875 was of much good. I didn't know enough about music to argue back, but I couldn't believe what he said was true. If that were true, I was facing a life of worship woe, having to lead worship for the rest of my career while having to bear music that I found only marginally inspiring.

What made the period of my life when I visited the contemporary, nondenominational church so wonderful was that I was visiting so many churches. I had taken a leave of absence from active ministry so that I could finish my Ph.D. I was traveling around a lot on Sundays, teaching classes in a variety of Presbyterian churches. When I wasn't teaching, I was visiting all sorts of worship services in a variety of settings: Roman Catholic, Charismatic, Episcopal, Lutheran, Methodist, Evangelical, Taizé, Greek Orthodox, and more. Over the years I have continued this practice of visiting different kinds of churches, now including worship in emergent churches. From each visit I have had the opportunity not only to see what different churches do, but also to look around and see how people have responded to what they do. As a counselor and psychologist at heart, I am always fascinated with people's experiences, especially with ones that make them healthier in all areas of life. Worship has a significant role in helping people become healthier by opening them to an encounter with God. My primary question has always been about what in worship makes that connection most powerful.

In my visits I have noticed a kind of sameness in most churches—a pedestrian sameness that suggests that most churches don't think much about how to connect people with God. Instead, many seem to have followed the belief that if they do what churches have always done, then the connection will be made automatically. This doesn't mean that the pastors don't try to make their sermons educational and inspirational or that music directors, musicians, and singers don't try to make their music excellent. What it means is that few churches seem to ask the key questions: does our worship help people experience God? Does our worship open people to the presence of Christ? Does our worship encourage people to become available to the Holy Spirit?

The fact that so many worship services seemed perfunctory has been discouraging to me over the years. Still, some church services have stood out. The ones that seemed to have the most vibrancy were also the ones that had the most *intentionality*. What I mean is that these were worship services in which the congregations obviously asked the questions above, or at least some form of them. They had broken away from doing things the *established* way and were attempting to create worship in an *intentional* way, a way that reflected a deep understanding of what tradition has attempted to do, what contemporary people are hungry for, what is going on in our culture, and how to connect the three. Church researcher Diana Butler Bass has talked about the differences between *intentional* congregations and those that merely do what has always been done. She says, "Intentional congregations are marked by mobility, choice, risk, reflexivity, and reflection. They think about what they do and why they do it in relation to their own history, their cultural context, the larger Christian story found in Scripture and liturgy, and in line with the longer traditions of Christian faith. In addition to *thinking about* their practices, they reflexively engage practices that best foster their sense of identity and mission."[1]

These intentional congregations are passionate in one thing. They want to restore the Holy to worship. They care deeply about people experiencing it, even if not every individual experiences it in every service. I believe that the passion to help people experience the Holy, however it is defined, is at the root of every form of worship. Every liturgy developed by every movement at one point was designed to help people experience the Holy.

The term *holy* is rooted in the Old English word *hal*. This is also the root of words such as *whole* and *health*. To be holy, whole, and healthy is to be one in body, mind, and spirit. Worship has the power to engage people in an experience of the Holy in a way that helps them become both whole and healthy. Congregations that seem best at restoring this experience are ones that are passionate about helping people grow spiritually through worship in a way that connects them to it in all of life.

Every liturgy was originally conceived with this passion at its center. Early Christian worship emerged out of synagogue practices, yet those traditions were modified in a way that integrated Greek practices, creating a new matrix that helped people experience the Holy. As Christianity became more integrated into Roman culture, aspects of Roman temple and political life enhanced the drama of Christian worship. During the time of the Reformation, after traditional Roman Catholic and Orthodox liturgy had become fixed in form, with little regard for how it inspired worshipers, the Reformers looked for ways to transform worship liturgies. They wanted worship to once again draw attention to the centrality of Scripture, full participation of the laity in the sacraments (as opposed to the medieval practice in which only clergy participated while laity watched), and the experience of Christ and the Holy Spirit through worship. During the post-Reformation age of the seventeenth century, other attempts to restore the Holy emerged through practices instituted by Methodists, Quakers, Shakers, Baptists, and many other newer Christian sects.

This same passion for restoring the Holy to worship has been a part of the evangelical and Pentecostal movements in America. Many congregations today, of all denominations, act with the same passion as they try to restore this experience to their worship while they continually transform worship. We see this all over: in the emergent church movement, in the continued growth of contemporary worship, and in mainline denominations as they seek to balance tradition and transformation. We may not always like what these movements have attempted to do, but they have a passion, and they never rest. They are always asking how to connect people with an experience of God through worship. And whenever they stop asking that question, others emerge to ask it and to provide new opportunities to encounter the Holy in a way that modifies tradition. The newest movement is the emergent church, at least among those in the postevangelical crowd. It is sparked by a passion for helping younger generations encounter Christ and will certainly be followed by another movement as future generations seek God in new ways through worship. Again, what all these movements have in common is that they are constantly and passionately trying to open people to an experience of God.

I have visited a number of churches in which this passion was evident. Some have been nondenominational. Some have been denominational. Some have been churches in which pastors wear robes, the sanctuaries have stained glass and candles, and the music is more traditional, yet they do everything with a nuanced flair that opens people to God. Other churches have been more contemporary but have not been so enamored with the contemporary style that they have forgotten the main point, which is to open people to an encounter with Christ. At the same time, I have visited many more churches where it was obvious that they are trying to imitate worship. What I mean is that they either try to maintain tradition by imitating the church of the past or they do contemporary worship in an attempt to imitate the trend of the day. Their worship lacks authenticity and inspiration.

So what is this book about? It is an attempt to restore intentionality and authenticity to worship in a way that will open people to the Holy. Not all people will resonate with our attempts at intentionality and authenticity. Many present churchgoers would rather imitate the church of the past or the trends of today. They don't care all that much about their own encounter with the Holy, and they really don't care about other people experiencing it. These are the people who make it hard for worship in congregations to be intentional and authentic. Often they are the people who run our church committees and threaten to leave or pull back their contributions when they don't get their way. They are the ones who keep churches from recreating worship in a way that restores a connection with God in worship. And they are a force. But I believe God is a greater force. This book is about how to open people to an encounter with the Holy in worship, how to follow God in this pursuit, and how to lead those who resist this experience.

This book offers congregations a pathway to intentionality in worship. In the following pages we will first explore the problem of worship in today's church. Then we will look at ways to reconceive worship with an emphasis on restoring the Holy to worship. Finally, we will look at pragmatic ways to lead a congregation to consider new ways of worshiping.

One final note: the kind of worship I will be advocating is one that I call an "integrated" approach. Terms such as *traditional*, *contemporary*, and *blended* are familiar. What I want to offer is an approach that leads to an integration of different elements.

You might be tempted to think that I am advocating blended worship. I am not. To me, blended worship is a style that mixes in all sorts of different elements to create a homogenization so that everyone can be happy. An integrated approach is different. It is not about blending but about maintaining the distinctiveness of each element of worship as a counterpoint to other elements. For instance, to take an integrated approach to worship means to intentionally choose music to create certain moods and effects that play off one another. An integrated approach to worship uses different modes of preaching, from traditional exposition to storytelling to multimedia presentations with PowerPoint slides and movie clips. It uses ritual in a way that opens people to multisensory experiences in worship. It also is willing to bring in elements from different denominations, movements, and even religions, when appropriate, in a way that enhances the encounter with Christ. It is intentionally integrative.

As we explore integrated worship together, I invite you to embark on this quest in prayer:

Holy Spirit, Christ, Creator, I want to worship you, . . . we want to worship you. Even more we want to experience you so that through our experiences we can give our whole selves to you. Help me to be a catalyst for leading others to encounter you in worship. And let my reading and reflections lead me to discover your calling to create a holy space in worship where all people can encounter, experience, and embrace you. In Christ's holy name I pray. Amen.

CHAPTER 1

———◆———

Where's the Holy?

ONE SUNDAY MORNING, A MOTHER WENT UPSTAIRS TO HER SON'S ROOM TO wake him for church. Slowly opening the door, as it softly squealed in protest, she said, "Dear, it's time to get up. It's time to go to church." The son grumbled and rolled over. Ten minutes later his mother again went up, opened the door, and said, "Dear, get up. It's time to go to church." He moaned and curled up tighter under the blankets, warding off the morning chill. Five minutes later she yelled, "Son! Get up!" His voice muffled by the blankets, he yelled back, "I don't want to go to church!" "You have to go to church!" she replied. "Why? Why do I have to go to church?" he protested.

The mother stepped back, paused, and said, "Three reasons. First, it's Sunday morning, and on Sunday mornings we go to church. Second, you're forty years old, and you're too old to be having this conversation with your mother. Third, you're the pastor of the church."

This story reflects how ambivalent so many pastors are about worship. The truth is that worship in many churches is boring. Too often it is uninspiring. Going to worship each Sunday can be a hassle. Why even bother with worship? Why is worship so essential to Christian faith? Can't people be Christians without worship? Many believe they can. They never go to church because they don't see the point. They say in a convincing way, "I don't need church. I find God in nature; in my children; in my friendships; in good food, laughter, and life. Getting up early on Sunday morning, dressing in uncomfortable clothes, sitting for an hour being bored, and then engaging in polite small talk with others just distracts me from God. What's wrong with finding

God on my own? I believe in God, and I pray. Why do I have to go to church, too?"

Still, millions of people attend worship every week, recognizing a correlation between spiritual growth and worship attendance. People often say to me that they feel better after going to church. Obviously, not everyone who goes to church is growing spiritually, especially since a number of churchgoers resist actual growth. But if you think about the most spiritually mature people you know, how many are regular churchgoers? My perspective as a pastor may be skewed, but I meet and talk to a lot of people, and I have met very few deeply spiritually mature people for whom worship isn't a priority. I am talking about people who manifest the fruit of the Spirit: "love, joy, peace, patience, kindness, generosity, faithfulness, gentleness, and self-control" (Gal. 5:22–23).

I have met a lot of people who say they are spiritual but not religious—dressing, acting, and speaking in ways that our culture seems to define as "spiritual." Most are good people, yet they seem to lack the level of maturity I see in the most spiritually mature Christians—Christians who connect worship and spiritual growth. Certainly many of these "spiritual but not religious" people are good people. But goodness and depth aren't the same thing. My point is simply that there is a direct correlation between worship attendance and spiritual maturity, yet we are still stuck with a basic problem: worship—don't always like it, can't be spiritually mature without it. Why? Because worship centers us in God's presence, grace, and will. It's for this reason that worship is the central act of every major religion. Get rid of worship and the church dies. As I have reminded staff members of our church, we can have worship without ministry and still be a church, but not ministry without worship. It is for all these reasons that the great spiritual figures of the Christian faith have always placed worship at the center of spiritual growth.

Why Do We Worship?

What is it about worship that nurtures spiritual maturity? The truth is that every aspect of worship nurtures spiritual maturity. The act of making a commitment to worship and making it a regular discipline increases our awareness of God and lessens our focus on ourselves. Engaging in worship practices such as sitting in sacred spaces, praising God in song, confessing, praying, listening, focusing our attention upon God, and reflecting on God's word all nurture spiritual growth. Unfortunately, so many people resist the holy power of worship because it threatens them at deeper levels. Worship is threatening because it is potentially transforming. The truth is that many people don't want to be transformed. They want to remain the same, to find that place in life where no changes are required and they can feel safe. So they resist the transforming power of worship. Of course, no one ever actually admits that they fear being transformed. Instead, they complain that the music is boring, that they don't like to sing, that they have to sit too long, that the service is too long or uninspiring, that the prayers are too long-winded, that the sanctuary is too formal, that the others there are too goody-two-shoes, or that they aren't goody-two-shoes enough and are hypocrites. There is a lot to complain about, but I think most of these complaints miss the real issue. The real issue is that too few people—whether they attend worship or avoid it—truly want to be transformed. In addition, a bigger problem looms: too few churches take seriously their call to be transforming, holy spaces where God can be discovered and met. Thus, the combination of people who fear transformation and churches that avoid transformation creates a void. What fills that void?

I understand all of these complaints on a very personal level. For most of my life I have really disliked worship. My wife tells me that if I weren't a pastor I would never go to worship. Fifteen years ago she was right about that, although I have managed to change over time. I am still not always that comfortable in worship in other churches. As a result I am always looking for ways to make worship more comfortable for others in my own church, which I hope will make it more comfortable for me. I am a constant tinkerer when it comes to designing worship. I am always working with our staff and members to figure out how to tweak our worship so that it will touch people and open them to what I think is paramount in a worship service: *encountering and experiencing God in a way that transforms us, even if just a little bit.* The ultimate end of worship is that it creates the conditions in which

Christ can live in us and us in him, in a way that reflects Jesus's call, "Abide in me as I abide in you. Just as the branch cannot bear fruit by itself unless it abides in the vine, neither can you unless you abide in me" (John 15:4).

The unfortunate reality is that, in North American society, neither the surrounding culture nor the church culture embraces the transforming encounter with God. Most mainline churches quit asking long ago whether our worship leads people to an encounter with Christ and the Holy Spirit. Think about why we do what we do in worship. Do we worship the way we do because it is how we have always done it? Do we worship the way we do because it is what we are best at? Do we worship the way we do because it makes certain members of the church happy? These reasons reside at the center of what has caused so many people to walk away from the church. Many people have wanted a tangible, transforming encounter with God but have never found it in worship, because worship has been focused on everything but that transforming encounter. It has failed to promote a receptivity in them that allows Christ to come alive in them. To foster an encounter with God means designing worship that is deliberately focused on making a spiritual and psychological impact on people. If people are to experience God in worship, it needs to resonate with where they are psychologically and spiritually. If mainline churches are rooted in a 1950s style of worship, or even a sixteenth-century style of worship, while trying to reach twenty-first-century people, why should we be surprised when people complain that they can't experience God in worship? If we don't offer people a venue through which they can access the spiritual, they will gladly find some other venue or ignore their spiritual yearnings and substitute the pursuits and pleasures of the world.

Why Do We Worship
the Way We Have Always Worshiped
When People Keep Changing?

The modern, mainline approach to worship is very different from the model of worship presented in Acts and in Paul's letters. The model offered by Paul is one that emphasizes adapting to where people in the local population are, rather than asking them to adapt to the church as it is. He says:

> For though I am free with respect to all, I have made myself a slave to all, so that I might win more of them. To the Jews I became as a Jew, in order to win Jews. To those under the law I became as one under the law (though I myself am not under the law) so that I might win those under the law. To those outside the law I became as one outside the law (though I am not free from God's law but am under Christ's law) so that I might win those outside the law. To the weak I became weak, so that I might win the weak. I have become all things to all people, that I might by all means save some. I do it all for the sake of the gospel, so that I may share in its blessings.
>
> —1 CORINTHIANS 9:19–23

In other words, Paul adapted himself to the people he was trying to reach. He adapted his speaking style. He adapted his actions. The early churches he founded weren't traditional synagogues like the ones he grew up in. They were some sort of hybrid between the Jewish synagogues and the Gentile temples, with crossbred ways of worship. He did not get rid of the Jewish ways of worship, which focused on singing psalms, praying, reading Scripture, and explaining Scripture. He adapted it by integrating Greek philosophical reasoning and other elements, such as sharing a meal, all so that the Gentiles could become a part of worship.

Christianity has been adapting for centuries. For instance, it's likely that Jesus was born in March or October, because Scripture says, "In that region there were shepherds living in the fields, keeping watch over their flock by night" (Luke 2:8). If the shepherds were out in the fields, then it was warm enough for the sheep to graze. Typically in December in the region of Judah the sheep would be indoors. So why does the Western church celebrate Christmas on December 25? Because that was the date the Romans celebrated the feast of Saturnalia, which was a huge celebration. Christians associated the birth of Jesus with an occasion that was already celebrated by the Romans and the

Greeks. Doing so allowed these new Christians to keep some of their cherished customs, while simultaneously adapting them to Christian beliefs.

In the late fourth and early fifth centuries, St. Patrick of Ireland did something similar when he brought Christianity to the island. Before Patrick opened the Celtic people to Christ, previous missionaries from the Roman Church had pretty much failed in their attempts. In fact, the Roman Church stopped sending missionaries because most had been killed by the Celts, a very insular people who distrusted outsiders. Patrick tried a new approach based on his experiences with the Celtic people after living among them for years. He knew the Celts, and he created a Christianity based on their cherished beliefs and customs.

Having grown up in the Roman province of Britannia in modern-day Wales, Patrick was himself of Roman-Anglo descent. When he was a young teen, a Celtic raiding party captured him, took him back to Ireland, and made him a slave. As a slave, he lived among the Celts for six years, tending sheep. When he finally escaped back to Britannia, he was a changed man. Celtic influences on his Romanized Christian faith helped him to see Christianity differently. He eventually became a priest, having been trained in Rome. In time he felt a calling to become a missionary to the Celtic people. Despite the reticence of the pope, he was named the Bishop of Ireland and given permission to lead a mission to the Celts. He returned to Ireland with a renewed vision. He would convert the Celts to Christianity, not by teaching a Romanized form of Christianity, but by creating a vibrant, Celtic form of Christianity.[1]

During that period, the Roman Church had a clear picture of how evangelism was to be done. Barbarians (anyone who wasn't part of the Roman Empire) were to be Romanized first in order to be Christianized. In other words, the church equated Roman civilization with Christian faith. They believed that to become Christian meant to become like a Roman citizen, which the Celts were never going to do. They were the antithesis of the Romans. They were a passionate, emotional people who embraced conflict rather than avoided it. When they entered battle, they went in naked, wearing nothing but sandals, a necklace, and a sword. They had no interest in reading or writing. And they saw Roman culture as a threat to their way of life. Therefore, missionaries trying to Romanize the Celts were usually beheaded or offered up to their gods in sacrifice.

Patrick had a new approach. He started by asking a basic question: What is essential to Christian faith, teaching, and worship, and how can it be adapted to the Celtic people? He stripped Christianity of its Roman trappings and formed a Celtic Christianity. For instance, instead of trying to teach about the Trinity in a doctrinaire way, he said to the Celts, "The Trinity is much like your beloved shamrock. Just as the shamrock is one plant with three leaves, God is one God with three persons. And God gave you the shamrock, which you cherish, to teach you about the Christian God." Patrick understood their love of nature, and so he created an expression of Christianity that embraced nature. The Celtic cross is an example of that. The Celts cherished the circle, which for them symbolized the sun. Patrick and his followers used the symbol of the circle to talk about God's unending love and presence in the world. They later integrated it into their version of the cross.

Patrick taught his followers well. For the next century, followers of Patrick's disciple Columba continued to spread Christianity among the Picts in Scotland. Later, following Columba's disciple Aidan, they spread Christianity to the Angles and Saxons in the now-abandoned (by the Roman Empire) province of Britannia. As researcher on Celtic evangelism and author George Hunter says:

> The mission of Aidan and his people represented the third major strategic adjustment in the history of Celtic expansion. Patrick and his people, who were Romanized Britons from England, had adapted their mission to fit the culture of the pagan Irish Celts. Columba and his people, all Irish, had adjusted to the somewhat different language and culture of the Celtic Picts in Scotland. Now Aidan and his entourage, most of them Irish, were in cross-cultural mission to the Germanic Anglo-Saxons now populating England—people with a very different language, culture, and primal religion. . . . Again, the missionaries labored to understand this very different population.[2]

Christianity has a rich history of adapting theological articulation, spiritual practices, symbols, and worship to new and different populations and generations. We in the mainline church have a hard time upholding that tradition, despite the fact that the Reformation of the sixteenth century was an adaptation of Christianity for a culture being transformed by the invention of the movable-type printing press, the growth of trade throughout Europe, and an increasing exchange of ideas. The Reformation adapted worship by creating a word-centered worship that challenged lay Christians to read and reflect on Scripture for themselves.

Why is it so important to adapt our worship? The answer is that the church has to adapt it because modern culture doesn't recognize the value of worship done as it was in generations past. Each generation is different in what it resonates with. They are different because over time the culture changes. The culture molds each succeeding generation as new technologies and ideas shape impressionable youth, yet each generation also molds the culture as it creates new trends. Thus, worship changes with each generation. Each succeeding generation develops a nuanced vocabulary, novel fashions, and new forms of music, and is tuned into an alternative set of experiences. Each generation redefines the culture. For instance, the parents of most baby boomers lived in isolation from other ethnicities, especially in the segregated South, and worship reflected that. Today's younger generations have become more open to different ethnic musical forms and have been more ethnically integrated but have tended to remain segregated racially. The generation emerging is much more open to actually integrating ethnicities and races. Each generation becomes like a new culture. The result is that worship rooted in previous generations loses its power to connect with each succeeding generation. Making the assumption that we can treat each generation the way we responded to the previous generation leads us to address spiritual questions that are no longer being asked, or at least not being asked in a way that can be addressed in forms familiar to today's older generations.

Take a cursory look at the current generations and how each one approaches worship. Those now in their seventies and eighties have had spiritual questions about security and stability.

They grew up during the Great Depression, World War II, and the Cold War, and their lives were marked by economic and military threats. So their cherished hymns and Scripture topics have had to do with striving for stability and community.

The generation now in its fifties and sixties has sought a sense of purpose, meaning, and fulfillment. They grew up during much more stable times, times that allowed for more self-focus and introspection, especially when compared to their parents' generation, which was so much more outwardly focused. At the same time, their youth was scarred by the Vietnam War and the assassinations of John F. Kennedy, Robert F. Kennedy, and Martin Luther King Jr. These events seemed so purposeless that they sparked a search for meaning and purpose. As a result, many have resonated with worship that leads people to develop a renewed sense of purpose.

The generation now in its thirties and forties has been seeking validation and relevance. They have spent most of their formative years being called "slackers," which has lead them to seek ways to legitimize their lives on their own terms. They have resonated with worship (when they have worshiped at all) that validates them no matter who they are or how they dress. Thus, many emergent churches catering to this generation meet them where they are, rather than asking them to adapt to where the church is.

The generation now in its teens and twenties resonates with worship emphasizing community and mission. My guess is that the worship that will become most meaningful for them will be worship that emphasizes unity and relationships, both locally and globally.

Each generation has different spiritual questions. Because we are so heavily influenced by older generations, we in the mainline church address all generations as though they are seeking security and stability. Or we focus on baby boomers' questions of purpose and meaning while ignoring the issues of generations seeking validation, relevance, community, and mission.

Part of the fallout of all these generational and cultural shifts is that worship slowly loses relevance for the generations ignored in our worship design. Too often the way we design and do worship fails to lead an increasingly diverse people to encounter God. It fails to help them tangibly experience Christ. The reality is that every renewal and reform movement of Christianity has intended to reach out to a diverse people who no longer encounter Christ through the church's worship and practices. For example, look at Christian history over the past five hundred years. The Reformation was largely a movement focused on allowing people to have a direct experience of Christ by inviting them to read and reflect on Scripture. It grew in response to the Roman Catholic belief that only trained clergy or monks were qualified to read and understand Scripture, meaning the laity were often barred from reading the Bible. Though the Reformation encouraged people to experience Christ directly through Scripture, sects developed different angles on the best ways to experience Christ, based on how they understood Scripture. Thus, each denomination tries to follow a model put forth in Scripture, or at least follow a model based on its interpretation of it.

Meanwhile, during the early Protestant period as the generations passed, several new movements cropped up in response to the limitations of the early Protestant movement. For example, the Reform movement in Geneva, Switzerland, developed many of its beliefs and practices in reaction to the Lutherans, Zwinglians, and Anabaptists. They offered a new path, but one that also had shortcomings. For instance, they offered an experience of Christ, but what about an experience of the Holy Spirit? The Quakers under George Fox, more than one hundred years later, and the Methodists under John Wesley, almost two hundred years later, recognized these limitations and adapted worship and faith practices to the questions of new generations in England. For instance, the Quakers created worship based on silence and waiting for the Spirit. The Methodists created an intensive small-group movement based on Bible reading and prayer that sought the guidance of the Spirit. Both Fox and Wesley recognized that the previous generation of church had become static and staid in worship, especially the Church of England, which they believed had lapsed too much into imitating the Roman Catholic form, and so they developed new practices. Adaptations ensued in following generations. The Shakers, who formed a much more emotional form of worship and practice, arose because they believed that their forebears, the Quakers, had lost their zeal and openness to God.

Most generations approach worship differently from previous ones. They are not always looking to reinvent worship, but they are seeking a renewed sense of relevance to their context. This continual spiritual seeking has given rise to Puritans and Presbyterians, evangelicals and fundamentalists, Pentecostals and New Agers.

Each generation has different yearnings, so the church is under constant pressure to adapt what it is doing to meet people where they are, while maintaining fidelity to the generations it has already been serving. This is a monumental task, made even more difficult because each new generation never really tells the previous generation what it is seeking, mainly because they aren't entirely sure themselves. Not knowing how to respond to the spiritual questions and yearnings of younger generations, the older generations have tended to criticize them as flighty, irresponsible, immature, and never quite as good as they themselves were and are. So, we in the church have to guess, experiment, and try our best to figure out what each generation is seeking. How do we adapt our worship when people keep changing?

Where Has the Holy Gone?

Ultimately, the problem isn't that each generation keeps changing. The problem is that as time passes congregations and their leaders forget to keep the focus of worship on the encounter with the Holy. They forget that unless people sense that they have had an encounter with Christ, an experience of the Spirit, and that through worship they are increasingly established in the Creator, then worship is no longer God-focused.

I believe that the main reason congregations neglect the Holy is that over time congregations slowly slip from a *spiritual* approach to worship to a *functional* approach. I wrote about this at length in one of my previous books, *Becoming a Blessed Church.*[3] What is the difference between the two? A functional approach to worship isn't concerned with leading people to experience the Holy. It aims to maintain what has always been done, to make members happy by keeping worship the same, and to design worship around the desires of longtime, traditional worshipers. The focus is on maintaining membership and the status quo. The proper function of worship matters much more than the experience of worship. A spiritual approach, in contrast, wants to help people gain a sense of the Creator's purpose in their lives, Christ's presence in worship, and the Spirit's power working through them.

No matter how spiritually vibrant a church may have been at one point in history, the attempt to maintain vibrancy by keeping alive traditions of any one generation eventually moves it from spiritual vibrancy to functionality. The irony is that the very attempt to stay vibrant by holding on to previous, life-giving modes of worship actually creates a functional worship that eventually drains it of its spiritual relevance. Maintaining passion in worship over the years is hard. It takes compelling leadership, a tremendous level of commitment by members, a clear sense of vision, and a willingness to adapt to new situations. When those four elements wane, the ensuing generations end up merely imitating the functions of worship and spiritual practices of previous generations. In their attempt to hold onto what was, they neglect the experience of the Holy that anchored the previous generations' worship. So they imitate the *forms* of worship that led people of the past to the Holy, while neglecting the *holy passion* that led to the creation of those forms. They choose function over connection with God, which causes them to neglect the experience of the Holy in worship. In effect, they just stop asking whether what they are doing is helping people to sense God's presence in worship.

This problem of functionality isn't a problem just for worship. It is also a problem for renewal and reformation movements in general. Think about the great reformers of the past. They had tremendous passion in their faith and practice. Unfortunately, their followers often focused on the functions of their practice, neglecting the spiritual experience the practice was meant to open people to. The inspirations arising out of the experiences were what led to particular reforms. They were reforming the church in the hope of leading people to similar experiences. If we look, for example, at John Calvin's life and approach to faith and worship, we see that he was never a Calvinist. Calvinism, which came after Calvin, was a movement centered on the function of Calvin's faith, but not the passion. For example, he wanted people to diligently and passionately read Scripture in order to become open to God's transforming voice in their lives. He wanted to free people from the church's rules in order to open them to the Spirit's guidance. Instead, many of his followers became consumed with creating new rules culled from Scripture. We see remnants of this in the Reformed churches, such as the Presbyterian Church (U.S.A.), which, in my experience, constantly emphasizes the need for order over ardor, saying that congregations need to do every thing "decently and in order." Calvin wanted ardor tempered by discipline, or order. In many ways, those of the Reform movement have inverted this by emphasizing order, thinking that ardor is somehow too emotional or pietistic.

Just as Calvin was never a Calvinist, Martin Luther was never a Lutheran, and John Wesley was never a Methodist. In fact, Jesus was never a Christian. The succeeding generations that followed the reformers' practices often forgot their passion. They forgot that the practices were created to open people up spiritually to avenues to God that had been blocked by the functionalism of previous generations. The ongoing problem of reform is that it attempts to break through a stifling orthodoxy (an accepted "right" dogma) and orthopraxy (an accepted "right" practice), yet once accepted, these new beliefs and practices become a new orthodoxy and orthopraxy. I believe the church experiences a constant tension between faith and function. When function becomes overbearing, people seek to discover new ways of expressing faith. And these new forms of faith develop their own new forms of function. With time the rigidity of function gives rise to a renewed faith, and a renewed faith to new function.

To put the problem simply, *churches shift from spirituality to functionality*. What is the difference between the two? *Functionality* means approaching life, tasks, and beliefs in an overly pragmatic, material, and worldly way. When functionality dominates our approach, we don't pay attention to the *qualities* that open people to an experience of God. Instead, we try to maintain the *practices* that have led to the experience. For instance, a functional approach to worship might be to look at it quantitatively (How many people showed up? How many people does the congregation need to show up for it to consider itself successful?) rather than qualitatively (How does a particular approach to worship affect people?).

Another example of functionality is how congregations approach the sacrament of communion. A functional approach emphasizes teaching people the "right" way to participate in communion or the "right" theological belief about communion, rather than helping people to open up to God during communion, allowing them to become open to Christ's presence, regardless of the manner or beliefs about communion. When our focus in communion is on right belief, right practice, and right distribution of the elements, we functionalize the experience. Are we doing it properly, the way it has always been done? We don't remember to ask whether people are experiencing God through it.

When spirituality characterizes our approach to life, we act in a way that emphasizes prayer, discernment, seeking the Creator's purpose in everything, experiencing Christ's incarnation everywhere, and sensing the Spirit's activity in everything everywhere. We emphasize a life in which people aspire to what God wants and are open to being inspired by the Spirit, and in which human reason and rationality serve our spiritual aspirations and inspirations. We make decisions based on what we sense God is calling us to do, what may lead us to discover and experience Christ, and what may inspire us to serve God in all areas of their lives. To bring this into the life of worship, an approach centered on spirituality doesn't focus so much on whether we are doing things the "right" way as it does on whether we are doing things in a way that reveals God and enables people to connect with God experientially.

However, we live in a largely functional culture that values proper analysis, objectivity, quantitative measures, and achievable outcomes. For many people this functional perspective is the default way of looking at life, one that religion often struggles against. There is nothing wrong with taking proper function into consideration in most parts of life, but when it comes to religious and spiritual life, functionality erodes people's ability to open up to the spiritual. Our culture rarely addresses the spiritual hunger in people, so people look for spiritual connection in anything that seems to offer it: astrology, fashion, nature, and so much more. In fact, one of the issues many of us in the mainline church recognize at a gut level when we are critical of the evangelical, megachurch movement is that it is something of a functional approach. While I am sure that many of these churches care deeply about leading people to Christ and genuinely lead people to an encounter with Christ, they are also often so market-driven that it leads them to develop a business-like functionality. Whether an evangelical or mainline church, if a congregation fails to offer an avenue that helps people connect with God, people will look elsewhere. The decline of the mainline church screams to us that our functionality has led people to silently leave our churches. In fact, considering our functionality, I often wonder why we haven't lost more members.

Worshiping in a functional way means adhering rigidly to tradition (whether that means in the order of worship or the instruments played in worship), preaching in a style reminiscent of sermons from the 1950s, or even following contemporary trends without ever asking if they are right for us. Functionality doesn't just mean doing things the way we have always done them. It means doing things based on questions such as, What will make people happy? What will increase our attendance? For example, many churches start contemporary worship services for functional reasons. They start them because that is what they see other, seemingly successful churches doing. What makes their approach functional rather than spiritual is that they never really ask whether the contemporary service is what God is calling them to do. They never ask whether a contemporary service in *their church* and in *their context* will help people experience the Holy. All they ask is whether contemporary worship will attract people to worship and increase their numbers. The calculation is based on quantitative measures, not qualitative ones.

Is there an alternative to the functional approach? The alternative is to try to restore the spiritual to people's lives through worship by becoming *intentional* about adapting worship to where people are spiritually. Adapting to where people are doesn't mean that we have to placate them. It is a question of simply taking down barriers that interfere with what we are trying to do. As I mentioned in this book's introduction, Diana Butler Bass, in her book *The Practicing Congregation*, talks about the importance of intentionality.[4] Being intentional means reassessing our practice of worship and asking whether what we are offering actually connects members of each generation with the Holy. It means asking a simple question: Do people encounter the Holy in our worship services?

The emergent church movement is an intentional movement that started as a reaction against the nondenominational, evangelical, contemporary, megachurch movement that grew so quickly throughout the 1980s and 1990s. The movement understands that a new generation of seekers is "emerging" and that they are seeking something more than worship as concert. What do I mean by "worship as concert"?

The contemporary worship movement arose as a reaction to what many of the younger generation of that time saw as the stagnation of mainline and fundamentalist churches of the 1950s and '60s. During the late 1970s, young evangelists recognized that rock concerts were the spiritual experiences of the baby boom generation. The touchstone concert experience was Woodstock in 1969, although during the late 1960s and 1970s, and even into the 1980s, any rock concert had spiritual overtones. I remember the summer my younger brother and sister followed the Grateful Dead, going to concerts all over the country. Afterwards they spoke of these concerts as spiritual experiences of love and inspiration, and one of them even said, "You know, if everyone went to a Grateful Dead concert once in their life, there would be peace on earth." Of course, my smart-aleck response was, "Do you mean before or after everyone took drugs?" But their point wasn't lost on me. Aren't churches hoping that people will experience love and inspiration in worship?

The emergent movement has been something of a post-Woodstock movement. The movement is hard to define because it is a reaction against the contemporary movement. It seems to integrate contemporary and traditional elements. Dan Kimball, a writer in this movement, says, "There is no emerging church model. I like to use the term 'approaches' to ministry rather than 'models.' In the future, there will be hundreds of hybrids of various approaches. Why? Because each local church is different."[5] So, what is emergent worship? Kimball says it is a move "away from a flat, two-dimensional form of worship in our gatherings. There is a definite move away from worship services simply composed of preaching and a few songs. We are now moving toward a much more multisensory approach comprised of many dimensions and expressions of worship."[6]

While Generation X also attended concerts, rock concerts weren't necessarily the exemplar spiritual experience of their generation. They generally have been a stimulation-seeking generation, finding it in extreme sports, video games, risk-taking activities, and music—starting with punk rock and moving through heavy metal. It seems that the alternative worship of the emergent movement, which started as a Gen X movement, sought to balance stimulation with meditation. Perhaps this generation was seeking more balance after a youth spent in stimulation. Whatever the reason, the emergent movement has reached this generation by reducing the level of stimulation and balancing it by offering a combination of contemporary and ancient practices. The generation has largely sought intimacy and authenticity in worship and spiritual matters.

So, have they had that peak spiritual experience akin to Woodstock? I think it has come through Starbucks. For many of them, the coffee shop experience that entails sitting in small groups, drinking coffee, and discussing life, politics, technology, and anything else has been a subtle, centering spiritual experience. Gen Xers have sought and found a certain sense of validation through relationships nurtured in small meeting places. Churches in the emergent movement understand this, so they try to create intimate, authentic worship.

Meanwhile, the evangelical movement is already starting to make the mistake that the mainstream movement made during the growth of the evangelical movement. The evangelical movement's growth is flattening statistically, and it may be facing a decline.[7] The response in many of these churches has been to double their efforts at what they have always done well: marketing, self-promotion, and bigger and better events. It worked in the past for the baby boom generation: offer bigger and better concerts. But what happens when a new generation seeks something different? What happens when they want authenticity and intimacy rather than performance and promotion?

Just as the contemporary movement was a response to the challenge of reaching baby boomers and the emergent movement was a response to the challenge of reaching Gen Xers (admittedly, there is crossover between the generations and the attempts to reach them), the mainline church faces a new challenge with a new generation. Another emerging generation in its teens and twenties is still seeking the spiritual in worship. Unfortunately, they aren't really telling us exactly what they want, but that is partly because they can't yet articulate what they seek. The issue for us is to intentionally ask how we can restore the Holy to worship for them and for us, so that they can experience God through worship. To do this means to become more *intentional* about emphasizing the *spiritual*.

To emphasize the spiritual in worship means to nurture an awareness that there is more to worship and worship practices than their function. To take a spiritual approach to worship means to explore, extract, and express a sense of meaning found in every element of worship, especially in the mundane aspects of worship. Bringing a spiritual perspective into it helps people transcend and reach beyond where they are. For instance, a spiritual approach to communion means teaching people how to take part in it in a way that helps them experience God, rather than a functional approach that treats communion as mere ritual, emphasizing right ways of practicing or believing. I am not suggesting that how churches practice communion is unimportant. What I am saying is that the attitude and perspective toward worship that churches nurture is important. Do we emphasize communion as a practice that connects people with the Creator? Do we emphasize it as a practice that awakens Christ within a person? Do we emphasize that when people take part in communion, they create space for the Spirit to enter? If so, how do we prepare people to experience God in communion? Do we treat the sacrament the way it has always been done? Are congregants reading words from a worship book written for previous generations? Do we find a way to update the language and practice of communion without losing its essence? These questions will be picked up in ensuing chapters, but the issue at the center is whether the spiritual or the functional is emphasized in communion and worship.

How Do We Communicate the Holy?

I have been considering generational differences throughout the chapter. What most people don't realize is that there are clear differences in the themes and issues each generation sees as imperative or inconsequential in life. As a result, each generation manifests what it holds to be imperatives in its fashion, recreational interests, music, literature, and even its adopted form of communication. For example, why have members of the baby boom generation tended to wear brightly colored clothes and those from Generation X dark clothes? What do these fashions say about their imperatives? Perhaps it reflects a generally optimistic perspective on the part of boomers and a more cynical perspective among Gen Xers. Does this play out when it comes to worship? In some ways it does. Baby boomers have tended to gravitate to worship spaces that are bright and colorful, while Gen Xers have tended to gravitate to worship spaces that are darker, emphasizing candlelight.[8] The challenge in restoring the Holy to worship is to recognize that different people experience the Holy in different ways. Churches cannot account for every difference, but they can become sensitive to these differences and adapt to them. For instance, can we create a lighting aesthetic that combines baby boomer and Gen Xer sensitivities?

The challenges churches face aren't new to the present age. Looking back one hundred years at the changes in communication styles demonstrates this. For instance, prior to the 1920s, the fundamental approach to sharing thoughts and ideas was through literature. People were used to reading or being read to. It was a common practice for people to gather around one person in the family who could read (literacy rates were lower), and listen to her or him read aloud a newspaper, book, or essay. As a result, ideas were largely articulated in a literary form, even when spoken. Thus, preaching was largely a practice of reading a treatise to people who concentrated hard as they listened. For instance, among the old-time Puritans of the seventeenth century, sermons typically lasted two hours, and often the congregation heard two sermons a day.[9] Pastoral prayers could last an hour.[10] For these people, a highly formalized, literary structure had the power to connect people with the Holy.

Reading aloud lost much of its power to connect people with the Holy beginning in the 1920s with the advent of the age of broadcast-style communication. What happened? In one word, *radio*. Radio changed everything. People listening to the radio were introduced to a much more familiar, narrative style of speaking, one that emphasized dramatic inflection of a voice over the turn of a phrase. The passion in a person's voice became as important as the structure of a sentence. Look at the popular religious radio personalities of the 1930s: Aimee Semple McPherson and Father Charles Coughlin. These evangelists used their dramatic voices to sway the nation. Radio is a medium best suited for communicating simple messages in dramatic ways. Even today radio is a powerful medium for both religious and political talk, especially when the message articulated is one from a more extreme perspective. Nuanced messages get lost on radio, but simplistic messages thrive. Complex messages thrived in a literary age in which people were willing to sit for long periods of time to pay attention. They withered in the age of radio because of its immediacy and emphasis on sound bites.

How did the rise of broadcast-style communication change how churches open people to the Divine? Religious movements that embraced this medium of communication thrived. Beginning in the 1920s, movements such as the Pentecostals that emphasized dramatic voice flourished. The mainline church went through a period of decline until it started to embrace a more oral style during the 1950s and 1960s. Still, as has often been the case with the mainline church, it often was caught between two worlds. Even as its pastors tried to adopt a more oral style that emphasized inflection, the structure of preaching remained very literary. Even today, that remains somewhat the case. Evangelical and Pentecostal pastors have been much quicker to embrace a broadcast style, preaching extemporaneously or with minimal notes, while most mainline pastors insist on preaching off a manuscript, often written in a literary style. Mainline pastors will read with great inflection, but they are still reading. Often their style of preaching is based on the turn of a phrase and the use of powerful voice inflection, tone, and timbre, whether the preacher is male or female. I am not saying these are inherently wrong. I am saying that they misfire a bit with generations who embrace other forms of communication and articulation.

Broadcast-style communication, especially as exemplified by radio personalities, remained the dominant form of communication for North American culture until the preeminence of television in the 1960s and 1970s. With the advent of television, communication became increasingly visual. Television changed everything. How people and events looked mattered as much as how they sounded. The use of images, visual symbols, and graphics on the television screen proliferated. Televangelists such as Pat Robertson and Jimmy Swaggart transformed the way many congregations worship. Increasingly, the emphasis shifted from how musicians and pastors sounded to how the worship space, singers, and pastors sounded *and* looked. Prior to the 1980s, the trend in many Protestant churches was to deemphasize art, images, and aesthetics in the sanctuary in order to keep people focused on the spoken word. For example, many sanctuaries had white walls and used muted colors for carpeting and woodwork.

In contrast, the evangelical movement of the 1980s and 1990s increasingly emphasized the visual—colors, images, and aesthetics. To worship in a nondenominational, evangelical megachurch is to be bombarded by visual imagery. For instance, I remember attending worship in one of these churches on a Fourth of July weekend several years ago. Two large PowerPoint screens displayed images of the U.S. flag flapping in the breeze, while every once in a while the slide would switch to show a bald eagle. Lyrics were projected on the screen. The pastors dressed in immaculate suits. The singers were dressed for success, sporting fashionable hairstyles and gold jewelry. The band was front and center, as the theatrical lights danced off their polished instruments. The worship space was much like a concert auditorium, constructed to de-emphasize everything in the space *except* what was taking place onstage. All eyes needed to be focused on the performance. In these churches the visual atmosphere matters, PowerPoint matters, lighting matters, being telegenic matters, being fashionable matters. These are folks who understand that they are reaching out to a visually oriented generation.

Meanwhile, so many mainline churches have resisted the change. We are still caught in the pre-twentieth-century religious insistence on stripping away all symbols and icons, believing them to be distractions (false idols?) from the Word. So many of our sanctuaries are visually subdued. I am not saying that they are ugly. I am saying that there is little visual stimulation. We don't take much account of what people see, thinking that all that matters is what people hear. How do we address generations that seek the Holy in what they see and not only in what they hear? How do we in the mainline church connect people with the Holy through the use of visual imagery? Do we even try? The mainline churches in the best position to reach out to a visual generation may be those from the Episcopal, Lutheran, Eastern Orthodox, or Roman Catholic traditions that have maintained a centuries-old appreciation for the power of symbols, icons, and images.

While we in the mainline church struggle to embrace visual modes of communication, the world is changing once again. A generation accustomed to visual images, yet seeking more, is emerging. In some ways, they want experiences that are less visual and more tangible. They want *multisensory experiences*. This is a generation raised on virtual-reality video games, a medium constantly striving to recreate reality through sight, touch, and sound. This is the Wii generation that seeks information not only through their eyes and ears but also through their fingers, noses, and tongues.

While above I suggested that the emergent movement is a Generation X movement, it would be more accurate to say that they are a late Generation X, early Millennial generation movement. Recognizing that they are reaching a multisensory generation, emergent churches use PowerPoint presentations, yet they use them differently than churches with contemporary worship use them. They use them less for projecting lyrics and more to restore missing symbols and icons to worship. It is quite common to go into the worship space of an emergent church and see on the screen pictures or short films of Celtic crosses in a cemetery, people holding hands, a crucifix, a stained-glass window, or hands holding a broken loaf of bread. The worship leaders are trying to engage people's imagination. The worship space itself is a contrast to the auditoriums of the evangelical movement. The lighting may be dim, which emphasizes the light of the candles placed all about the worship space, creating a multisensory experience of light. Musical styles range from ancient chants to traditional hymns to contemporary songs. Sharing in the sacrament of communion, a multisensory experience, is as central as preaching the Word. Small skits augment the sermon, bringing people into another experience of the Word. Sharing a communal meal afterwards is often as important as the worship itself. Holding hands during prayers or the benediction is common. The whole point is not just to hear or see but also to feel, smell, and taste—to experience.

How are we in the mainline church addressing these ways of communicating the Holy? Interestingly enough, I believe we are actually poised to take advantage of this new emphasis on multisensory communication because many of our churches are already multisensory, especially those that emphasize a sacramental liturgy such as Episcopalians, Lutherans, and Orthodox. We may be poised to be multisensory, but to be so still takes intentionality. Those of us in the Reformed or Methodist traditions may have a harder time because we don't always know what to do with sacraments or rituals. For example, those in the Reformed tradition could be accused of hoarding communion because of how seldom we celebrate the sacrament. We tend to believe that if we celebrate it too often, it loses its power to help people experience the Holy. With the generation coming into adulthood now, celebration of the Lord's Supper may have an enhanced ability to open people to an experience of the Divine. The arising generation seems to have an especial affinity for ritual. Many evangelical churches have recognized this. For instance, Eric Reed, a writer for *Christianity Today*, quotes a pastor who was asked about weekly communion and a recent trend in which churches were "returning to ritual": "We shouldn't reclaim liturgy because it 'works' in a postmodern age or because other churches are successful at it. We should do it because it reconnects us with historic Christianity and moves us from *my* spirituality to *our* spirituality, dating back 2,000 years."[11] Despite the pastor's assurances that all they are doing is reconnecting with historic Christianity, what he really is recognizing is that an arising generation wants to reconnect with historic Christianity through ritual. This is a departure from the previous generations.

So how do mainline churches "return to ritual"? During one of Calvin Presbyterian Church's worship services, we did so by creating a ritual connected to this verse: "Then Jesus told his disciples, 'If any want to become my followers, let them deny themselves and take up their cross and follow me'" (Matt. 16:24). Our worship—the hymns, prayers, and sermon—was designed around this passage. We bought small polished stone crosses that could be put in a pocket or on a necklace. We invited people to take part in a litany that included a minute of silence for people to offer to God in prayer what they would be willing to deny in order to follow Christ. Then we invited them to come forward and take a cross out of a small bowl—a tangible reminder that they are called to deny themselves, take up their crosses, and follow Christ. It was a simple, multisensory ritual. Unfortunately, many in mainline churches, however, fail to recognize the power that these kinds of rituals have.

What Do We Do Now?

The whole point of this chapter is that we in mainline churches have diminished our focus on the Holy in worship. This does not mean that no one in our churches actually experiences the Holy. No matter how functional, every church has people who bring personal passion to worship and who can encounter the Holy no matter what the worship service is like. Still, because our worship often lacks *intentionality* (an intentional focus on the Holy) in its design, we often fail to open connections for those who may have a budding spiritual passion for God.

I believe that many traditional Protestant churches have a misconception regarding how important it is for us to nurture spiritual passion in worshipers. Many people will say that the focus of everything in worship is on God, so the experience of the worshiper shouldn't matter. They say that all the hymns, the prayers, and even the sermon are for God. It is for this reason that they get upset when people clap in church after a particularly inspirational anthem or solo. They say that clapping puts too much emphasis on the performance and not enough on God. I disagree with all of this.

The power of worship is its ability to foster the relationship people have with God. Worship that is either completely God-focused or us-focused misses the mark. The most powerful worship actually is relationship-focused. It enhances the relationship between God and us. The hymns are selected not only to praise God but also to connect us with God. The prayers are said with appropriate inflection and passion that leads people to sense a bond between God and us. Preaching isn't so much an exploration of theological themes as an attempt to lift the veil of mystery separating us from God, as well as an invitation for people to discover how to live in divine union and love with God. Everything in worship should be designed to facilitate relationship with God. The question is, to what extent do churches have that sort of intentionality in our worship? To what extent are we adaptable to the needs of the people we are trying to reach? To what extent are we even aware of whom we are trying to reach?

Reflection Questions

1. To what extent would you say that people feel that they experience and encounter the Holy—Father, Son, and Holy Spirit—in your worship?

2. How intentional is your church's worship about trying to lead people to an encounter with the Holy?
3. How adaptable is your church? Is it willing to try new music, rituals, ways of praying, ways of preaching, or aesthetics to reach out to people, not only those of different generations but also of different lifestyles?
4. What are the obstacles in your worship and church that prevent you from helping people connect with God during worship?

CHAPTER 2

Tradition or Culture— Which One?

IF THE CHURCH IS CALLED TO OFFER MULTISENSORY WORSHIP, WHAT ARE WE supposed to do with our traditions? Don't traditions anchor our worship? How can we discard them so readily? Isn't one of the mainline church's strengths its ability to adhere to tradition in the face of a world that blindly chases trends? All of these questions are valid, but they are misleading, because often what we think of as traditions really aren't traditions at all.

Tradition and Retradition

It is certainly true that our faith traditions, and the forms they take, are essential to worship. Tradition links us with the source of faith. The practices, handed down across the ages, literally connect us with the original faith practices of Christ and his apostles. Taking part in these practices opens us to God by immersing us in sacred activities that help us become more available to God at our deepest levels—levels that go beyond conscious awareness. We in the mainline church inherently recognize how important tradition is to the life of faith, which is why we argue so aggressively about what to do with traditions—whether to keep, modify, or jettison them. Unfortunately, these fights over traditions also have the power to split churches.

For instance, the town where I grew up has two Presbyterian churches. One is the original church that started around 1835; the other is a church that split away from it in the late 1800s. Before the split, the original church was a thriving congregation. Then it decided to purchase an organ, which was the musical trend of the day. Up to that point, all music was sung a cappella according to the Reformed custom of the time. Many members believed that playing organs in worship was irreverent and against Presbyterian tradition. So they left that church to start their own church, one with no organ. Of course, twenty or so years later, guess what they installed in the sanctuary? An organ. Many churches still fight over organs today, but, ironically, now the fight is whether to get rid of them in favor of drums, guitars, and keyboards.

Why do churches like this one, and so many others today, fight so strenuously over tradition, only to give up their tradition a generation later? The answer is that they aren't fighting over traditions. They are fighting over *accretions*. People confuse accretions with traditions, and this confusion leads to worship wars.

The man who helped me understand the difference between traditions and accretions is Adrian van Kaam, a Roman Catholic priest and spiritual writer, with whom I studied in the early 1990s for my Ph.D in spiritual formation. Many of the insights I offer in this book are built on his prior insights about the spiritual life. Van Kaam may have been one of the greatest spiritual thinkers of the twentieth century. Unfortunately, he may go largely unknown because his writings are so dense and difficult to read. Still, studying with van Kaam and reading his writings was a revelation. One of those revelations was his understanding of the differences between *traditions* and *accretions*.

Van Kaam describes a tradition as the body of wisdom and practices that the church passes down from age to age. It connects us to the Holy. The particular practices we use in worship are what van Kaam calls *form traditions*. Form traditions are the set structure of practice, arising out of a faith tradition, that give meaning to our lives as we practice them. They bind us in faith with all who have come before us. They are the forms of practice that have been "handed over from generation to generation in a specific culture, religion, or ideology."[1] Basically, he is saying that participating in form-tradition practices has the power to connect us with God at a tangible, experiential level. The problem, according to van Kaam, is that these form traditions are easily confused with the "accretions" that slowly form around a tradition. According to van Kaam, we cannot be intentional about connecting with the Holy through our practices until we are able to distinguish between what is *accretional* and what is *foundational* to a tradition.[2]

We are not used to that word *accretional*. In its original meaning, an *accretion* is a buildup of sediment atop a rock formation or within water or soil. The sediment is not the foundation. It is the dirt, sand, or eroded minerals that accumulate over time. We confuse this junk with a foundation because it often either surrounds a foundation or is infused in it. When it comes to religious and spiritual practices, accretions are practices that build up around a tradition and become the ways a tradition is embodied in any day and age. For example, singing to God in worship is a foundational tradition. The songs we sing, which change from era to era, are the accretions. So singing is foundational, but whether we sing classical hymns, gospel, Taize chants, a cappella psalms, or contemporary songs, they are all accretions. Instrumental music in church is foundational, but the use of an organ is accretional. While pipe organs date back to the eighth century and have been used in cathedrals and churches for centuries, they really only came into widespread, common use in the United States between 1860 and 1920. Thus, they are part of our musical accretions, not our musical foundations.

The fact is that all religions, denominations, and congregations build new accretions atop old ones. Thus, each generation adds its own hymns and songs—and fights about them in the process. Sometimes alternative movements emerge in which a generation of adherents, disgruntled over the accretions that have built up and seem to obscure the original faith, try to strip away all the accretions and start anew. This is what contemporary worship attempted to do, beginning in the late 1960s, by creating a new form of worship. They hoped to get back to the foundational passion of the original church. The contemporary worship movement may seem like it is on the cutting edge, but the reality is that it has merely stripped away old accretions, replacing them with a new accretional layer atop the foundational tradition of music and singing in worship.

Why does the church fight over these accretions? We fight because we have become attached to them. We cherish them because they are in a form that is in sync with our generation, our culture, or both. They may be meaningful for us and for others of our generation, but they may not be meaningful for prior or ensuing generations, who see them as sacrilegious or archaic. And so we fight, believing our cherished accretions are the true tradition.

By now you may have come to the conclusion that accretions are bad and that we should somehow strive to seek only the purest of connections with the original tradition. Thinking this misses the point. The sediment that builds upon a foundation often is fertile soil out of which wonderful experiences can grow. However, this soil can also become shaky when centuries of accretions build up to the point that the foundation is inaccessible. As Jesus says, "I will show you what someone is like who comes to me, hears my words, and acts on them. That one is like a man building a house, who dug deeply and laid the foundation on rock; when a flood arose, the river burst against that house but could not shake it, because it had been well built. But the one who hears and does not act is like a man who built a house on the ground without a foundation. When the river burst against it, immediately it fell, and great was the ruin of that house" (Luke 6:47–49).

I realize that I am not applying this passage in its original sense, which is that we personally should build our lives on the solid foundation of Christ's teachings. Still, applying it to worship suggests that when we continually build worship upon accretions, without regard to the original foundations, we are building worship on shaky sand. We in the mainline church, who persist in building our worship on centuries of accretions, will continue to shrink until we decide to seriously question what is foundational or accretional about our worship, and then act accordingly.

What the mainline church needs to do is to refocus on what is foundational tradition—religiously, denominationally, and congregationally—and work our way back from there. Practicing an accretion is not wrong, as long as it is built on a meaningful foundation, as long as it is fertile soil for present generations and cultures, and as long as we are willing to brush it away when it becomes an impediment to growth. We need to ask, however, whether the practices we have built up—a focus on classical music, use of the organ, the literary forms we use when we read prayers and preach sermons, the anthems our choirs or ensembles sing, the way our sanctuaries look, and so much more—are fertile soil resting on a foundational tradition or shaky accretional sand that makes it hard to build upon a solid foundation.

If we are to restore the Holy to worship, we need to do something that Diana Butler Bass calls *retraditioning*.[3] Bass speaks of retraditioning throughout her book *The Practicing Congregation*, and until I read that word, I didn't realize that a term had been coined for sifting accretions from traditions. Retraditioning is what we have been trying to do at Calvin Presbyterian Church in Zelienople, Pennsylvania, over the past fourteen years. Retraditioning is the process of maintaining a church's roots in its foundational traditions, but in a way that makes the traditions relevant to a modern culture.

For example, at Calvin we have retraditioned the way we practice the sacrament of communion. First, by having communion every Sunday during our first service, we have restored the church to its Reformed foundations by pairing Word and Sacrament, which is rare for a Presbyterian church. Why celebrate communion each week? We recognized that many coming to our church were raised in traditions that practiced weekly communion, and that the practice has spiritual power for them because it was part of their tradition. We also knew that John Calvin, the preeminent voice of the Reformed movement (of which the Presbyterian tradition is a part), believed that every time the Word was preached, the Lord's Supper should be celebrated in response. Offering weekly communion both restored us to the original teaching of the Reformed movement and made our worship more relevant to people who have grown up with weekly communion.

Second, as we serve communion at Calvin Church, we offer both wine and juice. Over time we recognized that those who were raised in a tradition where wine was used (as opposed to the century-old Presbyterian tradition of using grape juice) feel as though something is missing when they drink juice instead.

Again, having both wine and juice maintains the accretion of using juice but restores the practice of using sacramental wine.

Third, trying to be more scriptural in our practice, we use a common loaf that we pass around as people tear off their own pieces, somewhat as the original disciples would have done. This symbolically takes us back to the scriptural account of communion in which a common loaf was used (although it also causes some to have to make a choice between their fear of germs and their faith in God).

Fourth, while I, as pastor, use the common Words of Institution during communion, I don't read aloud the prayers written in our denominational resources for communion. Why not? Most of those prayers are written in a literary style and seem stilted to people who are used to more effective, active, one-to-one oral communication. I speak much more extemporaneously, trying to be careful to use language typical of people today. I try to speak in a conversational way, employing contemporary word choices, sentence structures, and inflections. I try to make sure that my body and facial expression communicate, along with my words, what communion means. I smile and attempt to visually transmit a spiritual energy by trying to be a conduit for the Spirit's energy. In the introduction to communion, I often relate the sacrament to the sermon that has just been preached. For example, if I were using the passage cited above about building our house upon foundations of rock, I might say something like this:

> As we share in this sacrament, we are sharing in a holy moment that builds our lives upon a solid foundation. Sharing in this bread and this cup, we share the faith of Christ, who was determined to follow the Father's will no matter what. Jesus could easily have chosen another path, and he desperately wanted to take another path. While praying in the Garden of Gethsemane, Jesus was so afraid of going to the cross that he sweated blood. Yet he followed the Father's will. He had faith so that we could learn to have the same kind of faith. When you take part in this sacrament, you let this kind of faith grow in you. Christ is with us and in us, and by sharing in this sacrament, we let Christ become alive in and through us.

The Lord be with you.
Congregational response: *And also with you.*
Lift up your hearts.
We lift them up to the Lord our God.
Let us give thanks to the Lord our God.
It is right to give thanks and praise.

In addition, I emphasize the spirituality of communion, constantly explaining to the congregation that as we open up to Christ in the sacrament of communion, we create space for Christ's life and presence to grow within us, as well as space for the Spirit to work through us. I love to use the words of the Quaker writer Thomas Kelly, who says that the spirit of Christ lies slumbering within us, ready to be awakened by our simply saying yes to God.[4] I tell people that if we share in communion, even if we don't detect it, the Spirit is working in us to nourish us so that we can serve God throughout life. I remind them that it is not the power of their thoughts that makes communion powerful but the openness of their hearts and souls to God in communion.

What are we at Calvin Presbyterian doing by restoring weekly communion, reintroducing wine, using a common loaf, and using contemporary language? We are retraditioning the tradition. We have attempted to reroot our congregation in the original spiritual purpose of the tradition, while also asking how the tradition can be modified to speak to a multigenerational, multidenominational (at least in their roots) congregation.

To retradition worship, the church has to be sensitive to where people in our pews (or chairs) are coming from and then adapt what we do to where they are. This roots us in the tradition of St. Patrick, St. Columba, and Aidan that I spoke of in chapter 1. It roots us in the tradition of the apostles, who spread throughout the Roman Empire and beyond, adapting the nascent Christian faith to the people they encountered. Among Jews, the worship was Jewish. Among Gentiles, the worship was Gentile. When both were in a congregation, the worship integrated both perspectives.

Being Jewish with the Jews, Gentile with the Gentiles, and both with both leads us back to the whole point of this chapter.

In the mainline church, we have struggled to connect people with the Holy in worship because we have often failed to appreciate where people in our culture are in their thinking, their experiences, and their perceptions. We often blindly follow our denominational accretions, never wondering whether they still have the power to lead people to an encounter with Christ. We cannot assume that the practices of previous generations are adequate to reach out to new generations. At the same time, trying anything new to attract people runs the risk of dumping new accretional material on already shaky foundations. Just because something is new doesn't mean it is good.

Tradition or Trends?

In our zeal to retradition worship, we can become easily confused by the lure of trends. Too many church leaders, and especially pastors, confuse retraditioning with "trending" (following a trend regardless of its suitability and impact on a congregation). As I mentioned above, retraditioning means transforming a traditional practice in a way that actually enhances the experience of the tradition for a new generation. Trending means changing a traditional practice, or creating a new practice, for the main purpose of attracting people and making what the church does in worship easy for them. The latter is rooted in marketing. The former is rooted in discernment.

We confuse trending and retraditioning because on the surface there isn't much apparent difference between them. They both embrace meeting people where they are. They both try to be creative in reaching people. The difference between them is the exposure to the Holy that each one offers. When we follow a trend by instituting a new ritual or practice, people can become energized and excited because it stimulates them. Unfortunately, they confuse stimulation with inspiration, and mistake entertainment for enlightenment. Retraditioning has a different focus. It doesn't try to stimulate or energize people so much as it tries to access in them a deeper level of awareness. Retraditioning tries to reach people on a *transconscious* level.

Again, Adrian van Kaam developed a wonderful way of understanding this deeper awareness and connection. Just as psychology teaches that each of us has a conscious, preconscious, and subconscious mind, van Kaam says each person also has a *transconscious* mind, a deep level of consciousness that is always connected to God.[5] It is the level of the mind that God speaks to beyond our conscious awareness, which is why discernment always seems to come out of some deeper place within us. The practice of discernment is a practice aimed at accessing this transcendent level of consciousness through which we sense God's guidance rather than knowing with certainty. Van Kaam says that the transconscious "contains the aspirations and inspirations typical of a particular life-form."[6] To translate, he is saying is that this level of the mind is the place of our aspirations and inspirations. It is where we seek and discern God's will, a deep level of awareness where we are intuitively aware of God's voice and presence, even if we don't sense it consciously. Spiritually mature people seem to be consistently aware of God at a deep level, because they have intentionally tried to cultivate a constant connection with God through the transconscious. This is why these people seem to just "know" what God wants and is doing. Spiritually immature people generally have an atrophied or undeveloped transconsciousness that is detached from their consciousness. Their diminished level of awareness causes them either to follow conventional spiritual thinking (that can be conventional orthodox or New Age thinking) or to discount religion completely, saying confidently, "I'm spiritual but not religious," which leads to a spirituality with little practice. What they fail to understand is that religious practice enhances the connection much the way exercise enhances the body.

So what does all this have to do with retraditioning, worship, and the Holy? The power of traditional worship is that it enhances the link between the conscious and transconscious minds by engaging body, mind, and spirit in traditional practices and rituals that are designed to open people to God at this deep level. Worship engages the transconscious through sacrament, music, prayer, symbol, art, aesthetics, pace, and so much more. When we worship, a lot goes on beyond our conscious awareness.

Retraditioning enhances these transconscious connections for new generations and populations by making the tradition more accessible, forming a more powerful link between the conscious and transconscious minds. Trending has the ability to open this same connection, but only in small ways, either by masquerading as a practice rooted in tradition or by doing away with a tradition and substituting a "brand new" practice that is hip and exciting. It gives people the impression that by engaging in the practice, they are opening the connections all the way, while confining them instead to a more limited perspective that only partially opens their transconscious. Thus, the difference between the two is that retraditioning seeks to open an ever-deepening link between us and God, while trending seeks to stimulate people so that they will be attracted to God.

Let me give you an example of how the trending in a local megachurch seems to focus on stimulation that serves to attract. This church is adept at marketing in a way that many megachurches are. I have no problem with that, since they claim to reach the unchurched for Christ. What I do have a problem with is how they, in their zeal to attract people to worship, mistake trending for connecting people with God. For instance, on Good Friday, instead of offering Good Friday services, a deep tradition of Christianity (meant to help us understand the connection between suffering and faith, between taking up our crosses and following Christ), they host a 66,000 Easter egg hunt for children. You can sign your children up for either the 9:30 a.m. to noon event or the 1:30 to 4:00 p.m. event. That evening they hold the first of their seven Easter services, which stretch from Friday night through Sunday morning. They have gotten rid of the pain of Good Friday, a crucial part of understanding the cross, and concentrate only on the joy of Easter. Why? I can only speculate, but my guess is that Good Friday worship bums people out. Easter worship makes people happy. So they get rid of the bummer and emphasize the happy.

In addition, during Advent they host an open-house weekend during which, at each worship service, they raffle off to visitors a $1,000 Christmas shopping spree. When the local media asked them about it, they replied that they did it to reach people for

Christ, and that at their services 148 people gave their lives to Christ. They also said that one recipient of a spree gave it back to the church. On occasion they also give away Pittsburgh Steelers tickets to visitors who put their names in for a raffle on Sunday mornings. They have events for their youth group in which they raffle off iPod nanos to visiting youth. The question is, is this a case of retraditioning in which a congregation is adapting to the culture in order to reconnect people with the Holy, or is it an example of trending built on attractive but nonetheless accretional silt?

Retraditioning has one purpose: *to root people in a life-giving, Spirit-endowed tradition in a way that is accessible and opens them to God.* The question church leaders need to ask when considering how to retradition is, how we can transform a tradition in a new way that opens people to God's presence and power?

How to Retradition

Much of my initial interest in retraditioning (even if I didn't know the term yet) at Calvin Presbyterian Church was sparked by my studies of generational differences in churches. Prior to coming to Calvin Church, I constantly wondered why the mainline church was so terrible at reaching across different generations. This has been a personal question, since I am basically a late baby boomer or early Gen Xer (I was born at the end of one generation and the beginning of another) and felt very left out of the mainline worship tradition as a young worshiper, as a seminary student, and as an associate pastor. I eventually realized that the mainline church's problem was that we were so rooted in our accretions, which we mistook for traditions, that we had lost the ability to maintain what was holy while simultaneously reaching out to those of a different generation. So I became consumed with the question of how to retain the essential nature of our traditions while reaching out to those of my generation, to those who span the baby boom and Gen X generations.

While working on my doctorate in spiritual formation, I visited churches of all traditions, armed with the basic question, what makes this church successful or struggling? I visited traditional Congregational, Episcopalian, Lutheran, Methodist, and Presbyterian churches. I visited Pentecostal churches. I visited nondenominational evangelical churches. I visited Roman Catholic churches. I visited small, large, and medium-sized churches. I focused mainly on the elements that seemed to resonate the most—both with others as I observed their body language and with me at a gut level. A lot of churches seemed to focus mainly on maintenance of past practices or on performance, and those churches did little for me. But the ones that seemed to have the most impact were those that had deeply authentic elements. That doesn't mean the worship was authentic throughout. I have a hard time even defining what I mean by *authentic*. Authentic, to me, means that whatever was taking place seemed to genuinely connect people with a transconscious sense of God's presence.

What was authentic in the services I visited? I noticed how seriously some in the Catholic churches took their participation in communion and how the use of symbols such as the crucifix, candles, and albs enhanced the sacrament in a way that opened people to the Holy. I noticed in Episcopal churches how the use of architecture, candles, paraments, and atmosphere seemed to connote a warmth that naturally prepared people for God. I noticed how an invitation at the beginning of a Methodist service, in which the pastor told people that Christ stood at the door knocking, waiting for them to open it through worship, seemed to create a kind of holy anticipation in people. I noticed how, in a more contemporary church, the pastors got rid of formal instructions, such as "Please stand," "You may be seated," and "Please join me in prayer," and created a fluidity by moving from one worship event to another simply by launching into it. In a contemporary worship service I noticed how effectively a short pastoral prayer, spoken extemporaneously and with a sense of passion, drew the worshipers into the prayer in a way that longer, written prayers don't. I noticed in a small church how effective it could be to ask the congregation questions during a sermon and to mention people by name while giving examples of their experiences (for example, saying to a person, "John, what I'm talking about is just like what you do for a living . . ."). I noticed in a Taizé service how effective chanting could be. At a Catholic retreat center I noticed how powerful silence could be. Basically, I visited many places of worship, focusing on what churches were doing in worship and how it affected others and me, and then thought about how to integrate these elements into a Presbyterian worship service. I paid attention not only to Presbyterian traditions but also to those of other denominations. When I came to Calvin Church, I began to integrate into worship what I had learned.

Retraditioning isn't just a matter of reinterpreting the traditions of our particular church or denomination for a new time. It is also about reinterpreting traditions from other denominations for our context. In effect, we borrowed from everyone with one question in mind: *Will this help people at Calvin Church experience God?* I so believe in the idea of paying attention to what others are doing that our worship team travels one to two Sundays a year to visit other church worship services. Afterwards, we go to lunch and ask, "What can we adapt from this to our worship service? What did we find inspiring and touching? How do we re-create it in our context?"

When I came to Calvin Presbyterian Church in 1996, I sensed there were a significant number of areas where retraditioning might be called for: preaching, music, aesthetics, technology, and the pacing and tempo of the worship service. To give examples of retraditioning, let me share with you some of what we have done at Calvin Church.

Preaching

My first focus in preaching was to change the way I preached to allow it to become more available to others. In seminary I had been trained in a more literary style of preaching. I had learned to preach from manuscripts and to have my points all laid out in a linear, logical flow. After graduating from seminary I began to consider other ways of communicating. I spent time watching televangelists, ignoring what they said but paying attention to how they said it. I did the same with effective lecturers and speakers. I studied how they used their bodies, how they used their voices, how they organized their thoughts, and how they used stories, pictures, and objects to get their points across.

I wanted to learn how the most effective communicators communicated. The result was that I began to experiment with different ways of communicating. I might not only tell stories but I might also use objects to get a point across (for instance, I might use a geode to illustrate that what we see on the outside might obscure real beauty on the inside). I learned to use PowerPoint, not for projecting lyrics, but as a preaching tool to outline points, to create semi-Bible-study sermons as I moved line by line through a passage of Scripture, or to show pictures or charts. For instance, in one particular sermon about predestination, I spoke about how we confuse predestination with predetermination, the latter of which is a belief in fate and the idea that God controls everything, pulling all the strings. Predestination has to do with what our ultimate destiny is, whether it is salvation or damnation. I projected a map of Pennsylvania and New York, saying that predestination is much like traveling from Pittsburgh, Pennsylvania, to Olean, New York. Using a laser pointer I showed different routes I could take—the direct Interstate route, the back-roads route, the Great Lakes route, or the "head to California, cross the Pacific, cross Asia and Europe, cross the Atlantic, land in New York, rent a car, and drive to Olean" route. My point was that the destination is what God has decided, but that people have the freedom to respond by either following directly or going our own way. Using all of these elements—integrating the charisma of evangelical preachers, the clarity of lecturers, and experimenting with new technologies—I retraditioned my preaching.

MUSIC

Music is perhaps the most difficult area to retradition because it is where people most confuse tradition and accretion. Singing to God is the tradition. The style of music is the accretion. Knowing this frees churches to make intentional decisions about what music best reaches others. Knowing the difference also creates the context in which churches can decide whether to stay with a particular traditional accretion or choose a new form. The question, though, always has to take into consideration several factors. First, who are the people in our surrounding community, and what music are they likely to embrace, whether secular or sacred? Is this a community that likes country music? Hip-hop? Rhythm and blues? Jazz? Pop? Heavy Metal? Classical? A mix? Second, what kind of talent do we have in the church? Does it make sense to create a contemporary service if we can't do it well? Is that what God is calling us to do?

Eric Elnes, a United Church of Christ pastor, gets right to the heart of the issue of worship music by comparing it to how people listen to the radio.

> One day I was driving home from church listening to music on my car's CD player. As I continued to puzzle over our lack of youth involvement, a "plum fell from heaven," as the Buddhists say. The plum took the form of an inner observation: "Eric, this happens every week. You pull into church, turning off the rock or jazz on your CD player, then go inside and offer what you have to offer. Afterward, you pull away from church, turning back on your rock or jazz, and that's where it stays all week long."
>
> "Yes," I thought, "that's pretty accurate."
>
> Another plum fell, taking the form of a question: "Does the music you listen to all week move you spiritually?"
>
> "Yes, definitely," I responded. "If it didn't, I wouldn't be listening to it all week."
>
> A final plum fell, which I experienced more like a hand grenade: "If you're listening to this music all week long, and if it's moving you spiritually like you say, then why is there a firewall around worship? Why aren't you bringing it into the sanctuary, especially when your congregation isn't listening to 'church music' during the week either?"[7]

Retraditioning in music means understanding where people are musically and trying to choose music that touches where they are, while simultaneously transporting them to where they can experience God. What I mean is that our music shouldn't be chosen just because the style is one that people are accustomed to. It should also be chosen for its spiritual power to help people become open to the Divine. The question is not just how appealing a song is. It is also a matter of how well a song might help someone experience God.

When I came to Calvin Church, one of my first tasks was to assess where the congregation was musically. We were blessed with three talented musicians—Bruce Smith, the music director; Toni Schlemmer, the associate music director; and DeWayne Segafredo, an accompanist who was tremendous on the keyboards. All three had their own talents. Bruce's background was in classical, jazz, and show music; Toni's, in classical music and musical theater; and DeWayne's, in pop and alternative music. My first task was to encourage them to draw more on their musical interests. Early on I suggested to Bruce, who also played the organ, to play hymns and songs on the instruments for which they were written. For instance, "For All the Saints" seems to me to be a perfect organ hymn. "Amazing Grace" is better suited for piano, guitar, or fiddle. I suggested that the song should drive the choice of instruments. I also encouraged them all to choose songs in a wide variety of styles. I saw my role as supporting what they did, meaning that if they were criticized, I would take the heat for them. Also, my responsibility was to find ways to secure funds to help them purchase whatever instruments they needed to diversify our music. Sometimes the money just isn't available, which means that my role is to get us praying for what we sense we need from God, and then trusting that somehow God will find a way to make what we are praying for a possibility.

Retraditioning musically is a matter not just of getting the right instruments and encouraging musicians but also of trying to find what a congregation and the surrounding community resonates with. That means encouraging a combination of intentional change and experimentation. We experimented with contemporary worship, trying one service a month, but found that neither we worship leaders nor the church nor the community liked it much. We had the talent for it, but not the passion. So we decided to keep a base of traditional music while intentionally integrating contemporary, gospel, religious show tunes (from plays such as *Godspell* or *Jesus Christ Superstar*), blues, jazz, and other forms of music in our hymns, songs, and anthems. We also took our time making this transition, taking almost five years to really find the right mix.

Again, the point is that we retraditioned our music by recognizing what was important about the tradition of singing and music in worship, but also by recognizing that offering only traditional music was accretional. Intentionally retraditioning by adding new forms of music opened our congregation to God, while also attracting new members who were seeking this kind of authentic integration.

AESTHETICS

Another area where I saw a need for retraditioning was in the aesthetics of our sanctuary. When I came to Calvin Church, the sanctuary was a bit of a mess, having been neglected aesthetically for years. The church had gone through a period in which the leaders believed that money should mainly go to mission, not upkeep. (This is particularly irritating for me, because I believe that worship is where mission starts, and to neglect worship in favor of mission is like neglecting schools in order to focus on education.) The sanctuary had dim lighting, dark woodwork, wrinkled and stretched maroon carpeting, a choir loft with rickety folding chairs, and bare walls. It had lost its original aesthetic ability to connect people with the Holy.

I understood the theology of people who believed that money should go to mission rather than a building. There is an accretional strain in the Reformed tradition (a strain emanating from the beliefs of Ulrich Zwingli, who believed worship spaces should be rid of all distracting icons and idols) that says that any kind art in a sanctuary is a false idol. Yet the deeper Christian tradition, emerging out of the early synagogue and Temple traditions, recognized the connection between aesthetics and an experience of the Holy. My sense, when I came to Calvin Church, was that it was not treating the worship space as a sacred space.

So I believed one of the first tasks of retraditioning was to reintroduce art and religious symbols into the sanctuary in order to open people to the Sacred. When we embarked on renovating our sanctuary in 1998, I pushed the renovation team to consider the theology our aesthetics reflected. After a time of theological and spiritual discernment, the team decided to create a traditional setting with contemporary attributes. The new railings and woodwork would be a medium oak. Our keyboards, piano, and drums would be black. We would install theatrical lighting for our drama ministry, but it would be painted to match the color of the walls, thus not standing out.

Instead of following the Reformed accretion of banning all symbols, we have gone deeper into the tradition to choose artwork that is intended to inspire people and open them to God. We hung colorful quilted banners on the walls to bring color and religious symbols into the sanctuary. Over time we have also added replicas of ancient Celtic crosses that we have hung around the sanctuary. We also did little things, such as playing recorded meditative music throughout the sanctuary for thirty minutes prior to worship. We were intentional in trying to create a worship space that immersed people of all generations in a sense of the Sacred.

Principles of Retraditioning

What goes into the process of retraditioning? How do church leaders decide what to adapt and transform and what to maintain? I see at least seven basic principles to be kept in mind when deciding how to retradition in worship.

Principle 1: Know What a Tradition's Spiritual, Psychological, and Relational Purpose Is

Every worship tradition has a purpose. The purpose is always to experientially link a worshiper with the triune God in one way or another. The originators of a sacred practice were passionate about helping people experience the eternal realm, the ever-present kingdom of God that otherwise seems inaccessible. For instance, the point of the sacrament of the Lord's Supper isn't just to offer a ritual based on Jesus's death. The point is also to immerse people sacramentally in Jesus's death, resurrection, and subsequent incarnation in the world and us. Despite all the different denominational theologies regarding communion, its spiritual purpose is much the same: to open people to God at an experiential, transconscious level. The same is true of the practices of preaching, praying, singing, and listening.

The inherent problem is that too many churches don't take the time to try to understand their traditions. They either blindly follow the accretion of the tradition or eschew it in order to create something new and stimulating. I am not advocating massive historical research and documentation. What I am advocating is understanding what our deepest traditions are. To retradition means first to do the hard work of trying to understand what a tradition is trying to do spiritually, psychologically, and relationally, so that these foci can be maintained in any transformation of the tradition.

PRINCIPLE 2: KNOW YOUR OWN TRADITION BUT BE WILLING TO BORROW FROM OTHER TRADITIONS

Knowing our own traditions is always important, whether they be the more general Christian ones or those particular to our denomination. At the same time, exposing ourselves to other traditions and practices is important, because juxtaposing those with ours does two things. First, it helps us to become clearer about what our own traditions really are and how they differ from others'. Second, it exposes us to other ways of practicing a tradition, and thus helps us understand what may be traditional and what may be accretional.

Comparing our traditions to others' deepens our awareness of the power of our traditions. It also unleashes our creativity. Over the years I have learned that the truly creative people, especially geniuses, don't really create something new out of nothing. They integrate. They identify disparate ideas and find a way to bring them together. For instance, what made Pablo Picasso great wasn't that he created something completely new. He managed, instead, to integrate his classical art with new ideas emerging out of philosophy. He was the first great postmodern artist. He had the technical skill to create beautiful classical paintings, ones that viewed a subject from one perspective—that

of the observer standing at a fixed point outside the painting.
Instead, he chose to integrate a variety of observational perspectives. What do I mean by this? I will talk more about this in
chapter 4, but suffice it to say, Picasso's genius was that he realized all paintings are stuck representing one perspective, which
is the perspective of the viewer. He wanted to show many perspectives at once: frontal, side, top, interior, realistic, and even
imaginative perspectives.

At Calvin Church we are shameless borrowers. When we
find something that another church is doing that we sense might
heighten our members' spiritual experience, we integrate it into
our worship, while still being careful not to lose our essential
Reformed, Presbyterian identity.

PRINCIPLE 3: KNOW WHERE PEOPLE ARE SPIRITUALLY IN A MULTIDENOMINATIONAL, MULTITHEOLOGICAL WORLD

We live in a world that in many ways is much like the times of
Jesus and the apostles. During that time no one religion dominated. Even traditionally Jewish lands were multiethnic and multi-
religious. The farther one got from Jerusalem, the more this was
true. In Jesus's time there were Zoroastrians to the east in Persia,
worshipers of Osiris and Isis in Egypt, adherents of the Greek
gods throughout the Roman Empire, as well as Jews, Gnostics,
Stoics, Epicureans, and so many more. Jesus may have been a
Jew, but what made his teachings so incredible is that he integrated ideas from other belief systems while never losing his Jewish
roots. I don't want to suggest that all his teachings were merely
borrowed from other religious traditions, but if we understand
his times, we will find that strains of belief from the Gentile faiths
certainly seem to percolate through his teachings. For example,
look at his parable about Lazarus and the rich man.

> There was a rich man who was dressed in purple and fine linen
> and who feasted sumptuously every day. And at his gate lay a
> poor man named Lazarus, covered with sores, who longed to
> satisfy his hunger with what fell from the rich man's table; even
> the dogs would come and lick his sores. The poor man died and

was carried away by the angels to be with Abraham. The rich man also died and was buried. In Hades, where he was being tormented, he looked up and saw Abraham far away with Lazarus by his side. He called out, "Father Abraham, have mercy on me, and send Lazarus to dip the tip of his finger in water and cool my tongue; for I am in agony in these flames." But Abraham said, "Child, remember that during your lifetime you received your good things, and Lazarus in like manner evil things; but now he is comforted here, and you are in agony. Besides all this, between you and us a great chasm has been fixed, so that those who might want to pass from here to you cannot do so, and no one can cross from there to us." He said, "Then, father, I beg you to send him to my father's house—for I have five brothers—that he may warn them, so that they will not also come into this place of torment." Abraham replied, "They have Moses and the prophets; they should listen to them." He said, "No, father Abraham; but if someone goes to them from the dead, they will repent." He said to him, "If they do not listen to Moses and the prophets, neither will they be convinced even if someone rises from the dead."

—Luke 16:19–31

This parable is much more closely connected to Greek beliefs about the afterlife than Jewish ones. The Sadducees believed that there was no afterlife. The Pharisees believed in resurrection—the idea that when we die, we lie in the ground until the end times, when we are resurrected and given a new body. The parable above aligns much more closely to the then-contemporary Greek idea that the dead go to heaven or Hades. Jesus understood that he was speaking not just to people of the traditional Jewish faith but also to those who had been formed by the ideas of other faiths.

What does all this have to do with knowing where people are spiritually in our present culture? We live in a culture in which the adherents to a strict, orthodox Christian theology are few. Most people in our culture today have been or are raised with a mishmash of beliefs that span not only different denominational beliefs but also different religious and parareligious beliefs. Peo-

ple believe in everything from Christ to crystals. To retradition we
need to be sensitive to where people are and then to keep that in
mind as we transform traditions to meet people where they are.

Principle 4: Be Willing to Experiment—
to Succeed and to Fail

One of the lessons I have learned over the years is that if we are
afraid to fail, we will never succeed. Almost every great achieve-
ment has emerged out of failure. For example, Thomas Edison
went through hundreds of lightbulb prototypes before he found
a filament that worked. Abraham Lincoln lost the elections for
virtually every public office he ever sought, except one stint as
a congressman (after which he lost his reelection bid), before he
was elected president.

To succeed is to fail, even in worship. Creating a worship service that restores the Holy requires trying new things. It means
experimenting with different preaching styles, different kinds of
music, different ways of doing the sacraments, different ways of
praying. I don't believe in constant tinkering, because over time
that alienates people, creating resistance and a backlash from a
congregation. I believe that new experiments should be done ju-
diciously, always with the intent that they should be successful.
In fact, I have a simple formula for instituting change: *Make it
small and in the fall.* Introduce change in small steps and during
seasons when people are more open to change, such as fall or the
beginning of summer.

At Calvin Church, many of our experiments have worked. For
instance, we begin each worship service with a Taize-like chant
followed by thirty seconds of centering prayer. This replaced the
typical Presbyterian "call to worship" litany. We also offer thirty
seconds of silent prayer as part of the prayer of confession. We
replaced the traditional "Gloria" after the offering with a more
contemporary song, "Give Thanks." We introduced weekly communion during our first worship service. We introduced the use
of PowerPoint, not to project lyrics, but to post our announcements prior to the service and to use as an aid during sermons.
We have introduced all sorts of contemporary and nontraditional

songs, including songs we have written ourselves. (For samples, go to www.ngrahamstandish.org.)

Still, some of these experiments have failed. For instance, our contemporary services failed, and the staff and board of our church agreed to end them after only a couple of months because the staff grew weary of the heat we were getting from many members. We tried to introduce weekly communion during the second service, but the more traditional Presbyterians, who believe that communion should only be celebrated occasionally, were so negative toward it that we cut the experiment after only one month. Our church—staff, board, and members—has failed at many of our other experiments. The key is that when experimenting, the leaders of our church always keep an eye on how the experiments are affecting the congregation. If they become impediments rather than aids, then we have no problem discontinuing them, even if we wanted the changes.

PRINCIPLE 5: FOCUS ON CONNECTING PEOPLE WITH THE HOLY RATHER THAN ON WHAT YOU LIKE

This is a huge principle. One reason many pastors fail when they try to transform congregations is that they want these congregations to do what they want. In other words, these pastors have personal preferences that they want to include in worship. They fail because they try to create worship according to their own tastes. So, when the congregation resists, many pastors experience this resistance as a personal affront. The pastor sees the resistance as resistance to her or him.

I have led the effort to institute a lot of changes in our worship, but very rarely has it been to institute a practice that I passionately want. My focus has usually been on creating something I believe will help the congregation, and those we want to become part of the congregation, to experience God more fully. So when they resist the change, I am rarely offended. The truth is that if the congregation were to do the kind of worship I prefer, very few would worship in our church. I respond most to silence, meditative music, and stillness, with lots of candles and crosses. I like dark lighting that leads to centering. I like short sermons that really focus on a simple spiritual message. The problem is that most people don't respond as well to this. Most people want a combination of inspiration and entertainment. They want to feel centered, but they also want to experience "aha" moments. They want up-tempo or traditional songs. When we have offered services in the style I prefer, only about twenty people show up. They say they like it, but they don't stick.

The result is that I spend a lot of time trying to figure out where people are, and then considering how we can retradition in a way that opens them somewhat to the experiences I have whenever I am in a service that emphasizes stillness, centering, and meditation. But I don't force my preferences on them.

Principle 6: Be Creative but Also Pragmatic

Another reason many worship experiments fail is that they are often very creative but not pragmatic. When I have been on re-treats or at conferences, I have had the opportunity to experience lots of creative liturgies. However, while many of them are innovative, they often don't work well to open people to God's presence. In fact, many of them have been downright irritating and have actually inhibited an experience of the Holy. Why? Too often the designers never really considered how the ritual would work logistically, how the articulation would be experienced, or whether people were in the right place spiritually and psychologically to appreciate the ritual.

For example, I remember a service at a retreat in which a pastor led the congregation in a guided meditation during her sermon. The idea was fine, but the articulation was not. Typically, a guided meditation leads people to open up their spiritual imagination by leading them to envision being in places that calm them and open them to God. The leader uses a gentle voice to guide people, saying things like, "Imagine that you are in a warm place, a place where you sense God. Stand in that place. Feel the ground. Now imagine that you are opening your arms to God . . ." The problem with this particular guided meditation was that the pastor never gave anyone enough time to imagine. She would say, "Take time to be open to God in that space." She would then be quiet for five seconds and then move onto the next step. She also had a voice that wasn't calming. So the logistics and the articulation were poor.

Another problem is that sometimes the ideas may be creative, but they may also be bad ideas. Not all creative ideas are good ideas.

Basically, we need to ask not only what creatively opens people to God but also what works. This requires thinking through new rituals and approaches. It means really understanding the impact of what we do by imagining it from the perspectives of different kinds of people participating in it. It means thinking through everything—pacing, logistics, length of time, expectations, attention spans of participants—from perspectives other than our own. We need to consider a spiritual perspective: Will this ritual or practice actually connect people with God? We need to consider a psychological perspective: How will people experience it? We need to consider a relational perspective: Will this practice enhance relationships between God and worshipers, and among the worshipers themselves?

PRINCIPLE 7: BE PRAYERFUL IN SEEKING WHAT GOD WANTS

A final principle is that we should immerse retraditioning in what we sense God wants. It is not enough to understand what traditions are trying to do spiritually, borrow from other traditions, understand where others are spiritually, be willing to experiment, let go of what we want, and be creatively pragmatic. We also need to be prayerful, asking what God wants us to do. If we don't ask what God wants, then we end up serving our own needs and desires or those of our members.

One of the fundamental things we try to do when making changes at Calvin Church is to ask in prayer whether this change is something God is calling us to do. There have been times when we came up with what we thought was a great idea, but when we prayed about it, we sensed that God was saying either no or not yet. Listening for God is not easy at any time, but it is especially difficult when it affects something that we are already invested in doing. Also, how do we know if God is saying yes or no? There is no easy answer. It is beyond the scope of this chapter to discuss how we know what God is saying, but I have devoted many of my previous books, especially *Humble Leadership* and *Becoming a Blessed Church*, to these questions. Suffice to say, if we truly seek God's will in prayer, God finds a way of giving us an answer through either impressions on our hearts and minds or in the success or failure of our ventures.

Reflection Questions

1. As you reflect on the whole chapter, what concepts or points stood out for you and why?
2. Where do you see the tension between *traditions* and *accretions* cropping up in your church's worship, and how has your church resolved the tensions?
3. How has *retraditioning* either been or not been a part of your church's worship strategy, and what areas of worship could be retraditioned and how?
4. Where do you see the tension between *retraditioning* and *trending* in your church's worship, and how has your church tried to resolve these tensions?
5. How could your church creatively use the principle of retraditioning in its worship? Discuss ideas on specific areas of worship and brainstorm possible retraditioned practices.

CHAPTER 3

What Are We Trying to Do?

IT WAS THE LONGEST, MOST BORING WEDDING EVER. IRONICALLY, IT LASTED only fifteen minutes. I don't know if you have ever been to a wedding or a worship service like this one—I am willing to bet you have—but it would be hard to top it. What made it feel so long and boring? There was no sense of connection between us and the pastor and wedding party, or between God and us. It felt bereft of passion. Knowing the couple, I can attest that they definitely had a passion for each other, but the worship itself lacked a sense of spirit.

We were gathered in a small wooden church that was cute enough, I suppose, although it was obvious from the dingy carpet, worn pews, and dim lighting that the members of the church hadn't really paid much attention to the aesthetics of the sanctuary. Perhaps the church couldn't afford to fix it up. I am not sure what the reason was, but the atmosphere felt cheerless.

People were gathered in the pews, awaiting the beginning of the service. Without warning the bride, groom, and pastor were suddenly standing at the front—they must have walked up there without any procession. Not waiting for people to be quiet, the pastor started speaking: "We are gathered here today to witness the wedding of Joan and Dean, as they take their vows together in this holy place. Please join me in prayer." He spoke in a somewhat flat, uninspired voice. He went right from saying a prayer out of a book, to reading two passages of Scripture, to offering some very brief and uninspired words of guidance, to asking, "Do you take this woman to be your wife? Do you take this man to be your husband?" to saying the vows, to sharing the rings, to pronouncing them husband and wife, and then to saying, "Go in the name of the Father, Son, and Holy Spirit." Virtually without pausing, the pastor went from one part of the ceremony to the other, seemingly in one breath. I remember thinking afterwards, "What the heck just happened?"

The ceremony felt like it would never end while it was taking place, and when it ended, I wondered what happened to the actual wedding. What was the problem? The service definitely had all the essential elements of worship. It had a call to worship, prayer, Scripture reading, and a short homily. It had all the elements of a wedding—declaration of intent, vows, rings, pronouncement of marriage, and benediction. What was missing was spirit.

About a year later, I attended the greatest wedding ever. It was amazingly different from the wedding I just described. The wedding took place right after Christmas in an old stone Episcopal church with beautiful woodwork. The church was tastefully decorated with greens and candles, and the ceremony had a casual sort of pageantry. The priest was dressed in his robe and chasuble, and the bride and groom were appropriately dressed in their wedding finery. The prelude included classical music pieces ranging from Pachelbel to Bach played on an organ. The service started with a welcome from the priest and the congregation singing a hymn, "Joyful, Joyful." At this point you may be thinking, "Well, you just like a traditional service." But this is where the couple added several interesting elements to the service. After reading the Scripture and saying a prayer, the brother of the bride, playing a classical, flamenco-style guitar, sang "Groovy Kind of Love" in Italian. Normally, I find the song to be cheesy during those rare times I hear it on the radio, but when I heard it sung in Italian with Mediterranean-style guitar, it was beautiful. The priest's short homily was personal, cute, and touching all at the same time. The atmosphere of the church, the priest's personal touch, and the music set a joyful tone.

Then, as the bride and groom lit the unity candle and then stood to the side, her brother and a woman sang together the Beatles' song, "I Will." The way their sound resonated throughout the church was beautiful. The setting and their duet made the song come alive in a way that I had never sensed before. I honestly couldn't tell you how long the wedding took: perhaps an hour, perhaps an hour and a half. I have no idea, because I was absorbed in the worship.

Everything about the wedding connected me with something beyond, something divine, despite my resistance to it. You see, I wasn't expecting anything from the wedding. The bride and groom were friends of my wife's from college. I barely knew them, meaning that I had no real reason to expect a personal experience of connecting with God. So I was surprised to encounter Christ in that wedding.

What made the first wedding so blah, and the second one so wow? In short, the first one had all the right elements, but its focus was on doing what needed to be done for the bride and groom to be married. Its focus was functional, not spiritual. My sense is that the couple just wanted to get the wedding over with. Perhaps the reason is that the groom had been married before, and he didn't want all the hoopla that goes into a formal wedding. Whatever the reason, the wedding was *merely functional*.

In contrast, the second wedding was *intentionally spiritual*. In chapter 1, I talked about intentionality, saying that it means asking a simple question: Do people encounter the Holy in our worship services? Now, having remembered my saying this, you may get the wrong impression. I am not saying that singing "A Groovy Kind of Love" in Italian or "I Will" as a duet is spiritual. But the couple's intentionality in choosing these songs reflected their love and God's love. The aesthetics of the church were intentionally spiritual, and that intentionality reflected a congregation's desire to reveal an ancient connection with God through the building aesthetics. The decorations were intentionally spiritual, reflecting the liturgical season. The priest was intentionally spiritual in the way he spoke and interacted with the couple, the wedding party, and the congregation. The result was that, from my spiritually subjective point of view, this wedding allowed me to easily become open to the Divine and to turn a wedding for which I cared little beforehand into an encounter with the Holy.

The contrast between these two weddings leads to an important question for those of us reflecting on what makes for effective worship. Is our church's worship *merely functional* or *intention-*

ally spiritual? Are we trying to create worship that acts as a conduit, allowing people to experience an encounter with Christ, or are we creating worship that merely does what has always been done or what we think will get people to show up?

Spiritual versus Functional Worship

I introduced the differences between a spiritual and a functional approach in chapter 1. At the risk of being redundant, I want to go into more detail here, helping you to assess how your congregation worships. I believe one of the predominant reasons for the mainline church's decline over the past fifty years is that our worship has become overly functional. We have spent so much time trying to replicate the worship of the past that we have not asked whether it is still appropriate for the church of the present and future.

What is functional worship? It is worship that is more concerned with worshiping in a "right" or accepted way than a transforming way. This is a hard concept to get across, because even activities that are spiritual must have a functional form. To pray, people have to engage in functional practices. The difference is that when we do something spiritual, the way we function is designed to open ourselves to an encounter with the Holy. Function and form follows the Spirit. For example, prayer requires a certain function and form, but only insofar as it supports the spirit of prayer. We sit in a certain posture, breathe deeply, and fold our hands or place them in our laps. We adopt a certain form of prayer to release the spirit of prayer. If we were to be purely functional in prayer, our obsession would be with posture and placement of hands in a way that would actually inhibit prayer. It seems preposterous to become so focused on posture that we forget about prayer, but our churches can become so focused on the form of worship that we forget to actually worship God.

Worshipers and worship leaders can be guilty of several types of functionalism in worship: intellectual, traditional, and programmatic. *Intellectual functionalism* stresses human thinking over spiritual inspiration in preaching, praying, and practice. We in the Presbyterian tradition, as well as others in the Reformed tradition, seem to be most guilty of this intellectual functionalism, but we are not alone. Simply put, we Presbyterians live in our heads and fail to integrate our hearts and minds. We trivialize emotional expressions and experiences of God, as well as those who express them in worship. Our worst contempt is for those in the Pentecostal tradition, because "they just seem so, so . . . emotional." Intellectual functionalism is manifested most in worship through preaching that is disconnected from real life. This kind of preaching is speculative, focusing attention on abstract ideas and ideals, without clearly connecting them to lived experiences.

Again, intellectual functionalism is a bit difficult to explain in print. It is much easier to demonstrate. Still, elements of this approach can easily be recognized. In essence, preaching from this perspective assumes that transforming people is simply a matter of teaching them to think properly. It emphasizes theological thinking alone, as opposed to theological thinking coupled with spiritual and religious practices. It stresses rational analysis as the prominent pathways to God, while denying the importance of emotional, intuitive, and physical engagement. It trivializes piety, displays of affection, clapping, humor, and anything that smacks of emotionalism. It also tends to denigrate deeper ways of prayer, trivializing them as navel-gazing and introspection. It takes on an extreme rationalism in which only an orthodox theology matters, whether that be conservative or liberal.

There is little balance if the focus is on "thinking our way to God." Often intellectual functionalism, especially in Reformed worship, takes on a deeply Calvinistic encratism. What is *encratism*? The term comes from a second-century, semi-Christian sect called the Encratites, who had a very severe approach to faith focused on abstinence and suffering as a pathway to God. They forbade marriage, abstained from meat and alcohol, and focused on living as frugally and sparely as possible, believing that doing so unlocks their spirit to ascend to the divine realm. Modern encratism is an austere approach to faith and practice that concentrates unduly on our sinful nature and the need to be purged of all sinful thoughts so that they can be replaced by only pure knowledge and beliefs. The focus is on developing theological purity as a path to salvation. As Urban Holmes, an Episcopal priest and theologian, points out, it often accompanies a more intellectual, speculative approach to faith and worship.[1] The belief is that by being austere and purging their worship of all emotion and false idols, while simultaneously focusing on the teaching of pure doctrine, people can unleash their spirits to focus more on God. Ultimately, an intellectual functionalism in worship diminishes the importance of every element in worship other than the reading of Scripture and preaching.

What would this kind of preaching sound like? An example might be preaching about the cross without making the connection between Jesus's sacrifice on the cross and how people live their daily lives. It might also be preaching about theological concepts such as the Trinity, salvation, atonement, redemption, heresies, or any other theological topic in an overly abstract, speculative, disconnected way. It means preaching about God in a way that severs God from daily life, suggesting that God gave us brains and expects us to use them, so don't bother God too much with our problems. Just make sure you have the right beliefs and theology, and you will be fine.

Traditional functionalism is a bit different. Just as intellectual functionalism prizes rational, analytical thought, traditional functionalism values maintaining established practices at all costs. We most often see such functionalism in the Roman Catholic, Orthodox, and Anglican communities, but it can be present in any tradition. When we take this approach to worship, all that matters is linking the present with the past. These traditions often have a strong hierarchy that squelches new expressions of faith in worship. The focus is on a sense of liturgical security. Leaders never question whether worship is opening people spiritually. The basic assumption is that if we uphold our tradition, it will automatically open people to God. We unquestioningly maintain tradition—saying liturgical prayers, singing traditional hymns, and preaching in traditional ways—because we assume that a connection with God is formed through it. Or worse, we don't particularly care about the connection. All that matters is functioning the way we have for hundreds, if not thousands, of years.

A third kind of functionality, *programmatic*, is just now emerging and afflicts many new evangelical megachurches as well as those that aspire to that form of growth. These churches have often excelled at taking risks in their attempts to connect worshipers spiritually with God. The problem with this approach is that their success breeds a self-gratifying form of functionalism. Proponents' consuming passion is finding ways to attract people where they are. Basing much of what they do on marketing and business principles, they are always looking for what works, and as soon as something appears to work, they standardize it. Often their focus is not so much on what inspires worshipers as on what grabs, stimulates, or entertains them.

These churches pay great attention to what works in other churches. If a new practice, song, style of preaching, use of technology, or worship program attracts worshipers in one church, others quickly imitate it. What makes it functional is that the imitators aren't necessarily asking if this new approach opens people to the Holy. The basic question is whether it attracts worshipers.

So what? Aren't approaches that attract people to worship the same as holy practices? Aren't these people coming to worship because they are experiencing the Holy? Not necessarily. They could be attracted only to the entertainment value of this kind of worship. Just because scads of people go to sporting events, rock concerts, movies, and plays doesn't mean that they are having inherently spiritual experiences. People are often attracted to gatherings for reasons other than spiritual experience. For instance, a new member to our church told me about her experience in a local megachurch. She said that she didn't like the service much, but she appreciated the case of Krispy Kreme doughnuts she was given at the door as she left, all because she was a visitor that Sunday.

The point is that functional worship diminishes the encounter with God, whether by emphasizing a disconnected intellectualism, adhering to traditions that may not have meaning in a present context, or creating standardized programs that focus more on attraction than on inspiration. And this diminishment can take place in denominational or nondenominational churches, traditional or contemporary churches, or Protestant, Orthodox, or Catholic churches.

The contrast to functional worship is *intentionally spiritual* worship, but even this term is a bit confusing, because the spiritual has a functional element, as was mentioned above. Worship has structure, and structure is functional. The difference is that in spiritual worship, the functional serves the spiritual quest of helping people become open to the Divine. In functional worship, worship serves the functional quest of making people happy by playing their favorite hymns, imitating a rock concert, or maintaining the status quo by doing what has always been done. Ultimately, functional worship always serves the basic question, What will get people to show up?

The question at the heart of spiritually focused worship is whether the intent of the worship is to enhance the connection between the worshiper and the Divine. Worship is a conduit. It is meant to be a time in which people become open to the voice and presence of Christ. As Paul says, "when one turns to the Lord, the veil is removed" (2 Cor. 3:16). The veil between the kingdom of earth and the kingdom of heaven is lifted, allowing people to experience the kingdom of God. When both the worship and the worshiper are passionately intentional about experiencing God, the kingdom of heaven permeates the earthly. The key is that, while the veil can be lifted in any form of worship if the worshiper is willing to work toward that end, spiritual intentionality enhances the natural connection between worshiper and God.

I find it much easier to explain the functional than the spiritual because, as subjective as the functional can be, spiritual worship is even more subjective. Why? Because even functional worship can be spiritual for the worshiper who is determined to experience God. For such people, functional (or even dysfunctional) worship might not impede the process. The unfortunate reality is that only a small fraction of people come to worship determined to find the spiritual no matter what. Most people need a bit of help, which is the whole reason we are exploring restoring the Holy to worship.

So, if we hope to restore the Holy to worship by stressing the spiritual over the functional, how are we to understand *spiritual*? There are lots of long and complicated definitions for the term *spiritual*. It is a hard concept to capture in rational terms. Spiritual experiences aren't necessarily rational. They are whole-being experiences that include cognition, emotion, perception, and all sorts of deeper ways of experiencing life. The functional, by and large, tends to emphasize just one kind of experience—intellectual or emotional or contemporary or traditional. By doing so, it keeps people more on the surface of faith, rather than taking them deeper. It emphasizes order, clarity, comfort, and security. Spirituality emphasizes an integration of senses that leads to a heightened and transforming experience of God's presence in life. The key in any spiritual endeavor or experience is that it leads people to be transformed by God, even if in only the smallest, least noticeable ways. We become transformed because any true contact with God inevitably transforms us. Think of Moses on the mountain, who, after forty days of communing with God, returned to the people. When he did, we hear, "As he came down from the mountain with the two tablets of the covenant in his hand, Moses did not know that the skin of his face shone because he had been talking with God" (Ex. 34:29).

Worship is meant to transform us, although rarely as dramatically as Moses. Any spiritual encounter transforms us. Literally thousands of books have been written over the centuries by mystics emphasizing the transforming nature of spiritual encounters with God. Intentionally spiritual worship facilitates this encounter, and thus this transformation.

C. S. Lewis, in his book *Mere Christianity*, summarizes the thinking of all those mystics who came before him:

> The Christian way is different: harder and easier. Christ says, "Give me All. I don't want so much of your time and so much of your money and so much of your work: I want You. I have not come to torment your natural self, but to kill it. No half-measures are any good. I don't want to cut off a branch here and a branch there, I want to have the whole tree down. Hand over the whole natural self, all the desires which you think innocent as well as the ones you think wicked—the whole outfit. I will give you a new self instead. In fact, I will give you Myself: my own will shall become yours."[2]

Obviously, people aren't going to change that much each week in worship, but worship should contribute to this kind of transformation and sanctification each week. Weekly worship leads to cumulative transformation.

The center of the church's practices is worship, and of the church Lewis says, "In the same way the Church exists for nothing else but to draw men into Christ, to make them little Christs. If they are not doing that, all the cathedrals, clergy, missions, sermons, even the Bible itself, are simply a waste of time."[3] If our worship isn't at least attempting to transform people into to "little Christs," then aren't we in the church wasting our time? The difference between spiritual and functional worship is that the spiritual is passionate about transformation. The functional is only passionate about imitation—imitating the practices of the past or the successes of others in the present.

Information versus Formation in Worship

Foundational to the question of whether worship is functional or spiritual is the question of whether it is informational or formational. To be *informational* in worship leads to functionality, while to be *formational* leads to spirituality. Yet these terms are not just synonyms for *functional* and *spiritual* respectively. While an informative approach to worship leads to functionality, information can still serve formation and thus lead to an enhanced spiritual openness in worship.

Let's start with what the two terms mean. To be *informational* means to focus on information about a subject rather than engaging it in a way that shapes and forms our lives. Informational thinking stresses facts, data, and the basics of a topic that feed the intellectual sphere while failing to connect it with practical life. Mainline churches in general have largely developed an informational approach to faith in preaching and teaching, and we can see its influence throughout worship. Not only our sermons but also our worship songs and prayers are informational. What that means is that they tell us about God, faith, and life in the abstract, but they don't necessarily connect this information with the realities of living a more spiritually vibrant life.

Information by itself does not lead to transformation. When we approach anything informationally, our goal is to consume the information because we find it interesting, entertaining, or useful to pass a test or complete a project. Information doesn't transform us, because it leads us to think *about* God rather than engage *with* God. To better understand what I mean by the distinction, we need to first define the *formational* approach.

When people live life in a formative way, they combine logic, emotion, and intuition, with Scripture, prayer, reflection, and discernment. For example, formative teachers use information in their teaching in a way that allows people to become transformed in the process of learning it. When preachers are formative in worship, they invite people to spiritually reflect on theological and religious information, as well as life events, in order to allow the Spirit to speak in ways that guide people's lives. They invite worshipers to reflectively ask, "What does this experience say to me about my life? How is God speaking to me through this sermon, prayer, song, or worship service? How is God calling me to change my life in response to what I've heard in Scripture or the sermon? How do I apply what I'm sensing to my life in a practical, tangible way?"

Just as the functional can serve the spiritual but the spiritual can't serve the functional, information can serve formation but formation cannot serve information. Why not? Because the goal of formation is to transform and reform people by opening them to an encounter with Christ, while the goal of information is to learn concepts, facts, and data, whether or not they have any impact on how people live. How do information and formation intersect in worship, and how do they nurture either functionality or spirituality? Let's take a look more specifically at how information and formation interact in the elements of worship.

PREACHING

The most obvious aspect of worship where information and formation conflict is in preaching. It is so easy to emphasize an informational approach over a formational one, mainly because many pastors in the mainline church have been steeped in the historical-critical method of biblical interpretation, which is an informational-functional approach to the Bible. This method interprets the Bible as a text created by human beings in a particular historical era rather than the inerrant word of God. It values Scripture as the authoritative and inspired word of God, but it is cautious about inerrancy. It does so by studying the historical context and culture of the period when the passage was written. It then attempts to interpret Scripture in light of understanding who wrote the passage, what their motives were, what biases they might have had, what they were trying to say, and who they were trying to say it to. It treats biblical passages as information to be dissected and understood.

Now, before you get defensive about the method, thinking that I am saying that the historical-critical method of biblical interpretation is bad or somehow wrong, understand my point. It is not inherently bad, but it does investigate Scripture informationally, and when used as the sole basis for creating sermons, it can cause the sermons to become informational and functional. In other words, the historical-critical method needs to be balanced by a spiritual-reflective reading of Scripture. The historical-critical method can supplement a spiritual reading of Scripture, but it can't substitute for it. In other words, historical-critical information can serve formation, but not the other way around.

The problem with the historical-critical method is that it is consumed with informational tasks such as figuring out who wrote a passage and why. Meanwhile, the formative questions are: What difference does this make in my life, what is God saying to me through it, and how can I apply it to my life in a way that draws me closer to God? The information discovered through historical-critical exploration can lead one into a more formative approach, but not always. It depends upon how open to formation the preacher or researcher is. I believe the historical-critical method helps us understand the Bible better. But I don't believe in relying on it as the sole basis for preaching. I believe that the information gleaned from this method needs to lead to a formative application to life that leads to a transformation of life.

So, what do informational and formational sermons look like? Informational sermons treat subjects in an abstract and speculative way that disconnects concepts from our own lives. For example, an informational sermon might tell us about Jesus's life, telling us about how Jesus died for our sins on the cross, exploring themes such as love, forgiveness, prayer, healing, faith, and calling in the abstract, giving us all sorts of theological and technical concepts and constructs about these subjects. Formative sermons tell us how to pragmatically employ them in our lives. Often, stories serve a formative function in sermons, giving a formative explication of a technical concept. They teach theology in a way that shows people how to live this theology pragmatically to transform life.

Let me give you an example. The following is a nice, short, informational sermon on Paul's statement in Romans 3:23–24 that all have sinned and fall short of the glory of God and are justified freely by his grace through the redemption that came by Christ Jesus. It would be acceptable in many churches:

> Understand that Paul is saying we are saved by grace. We are saved by the redeeming power of Christ. God no longer holds our sin against us. We are freed from the shackles of sin and are now free to live in that grace. And our faith opens us to this possibility.

Nothing wrong with that sermon except that it is informational, because it tells us about faith in the abstract and in a way that can leave us saying, "So what? What does that have to do with the problems I have in my life now?" How do we make it more formational?

The information provided in the passage from Romans is important. It is foundational for the Christian life. The formative question is, how can the church use this information to form and transform lives? This question is about more than just application. Application is important, but formation goes deeper. Information is meant to be used as a catalyst for transforming and reforming life. Application implies acting in a certain way that helps solve or resolve problems. To make the sermon more formative requires simply answering the question, how does what we are doing in worship enable people to connect with God in a way that makes a tangible, experiential difference in their lives? For example, a formative version of the same sermon might say:

Understand that Paul is saying we are saved by grace. We are saved by the redeeming power of Christ. God no longer holds our sin against us. We are freed from the shackles of sin and are now free to live in that grace. And our faith opens us to this possibility. [Here is the formative part:] So you're now asking, "What difference does this make in my life?" It makes a lot of difference. What it says is that God's grace is now available to you in every moment of life. For example, if you are in a conflict with someone at work, there may be ways of resolving it through prayer. If you can slow down, pray inwardly, and become open to God in the very moment of conflict, truly asking God to show you how to make this situation better or to resolve a conflict, God's grace has the power to bring you to an answer. If you find yourself in a conflict, try stepping back and asking God to work in and through you. I have a friend who did this. He told me that he was in a meeting where people were yelling at one another over some hotly contested issue. He spoke up and said, "Hey, can we just cool down and sit in silence for a moment?" During that moment of quiet, he silently prayed for God to guide them. And when they started talking again, a different spirit was in the air. All of a sudden they started cooperating. That's the difference grace makes. You aren't only saved by this grace, but if you have faith—if you are willing to really trust in God in every moment—you may find that this grace can now flow through you and help change your life as well as others'.

What made this formative is that the information was placed in a context that could now shape, form, transform, and reform lives.

Liturgical Prayers

Perhaps some of the most functional, informational parts of the worship service are the prayers. This is because prayers are the more formal part in many worship services. For whatever reason, there seems to be a tradition in the mainline church to use stilted language, passive verbs, and lengthy sentence constructions. In other words, prayers are often written with loftiness rather than formation in mind. Again, how to overcome this loftiness is hard to convey, because we are used to a more wooden style of praying in the mainline church. Probably this has a lot to do with our using traditional books of common worship or prayer that emerge out of previous centuries. The language is often beautiful, perhaps even poetic, but it can also become more informational because it fails to connect people experientially with God. Liturgical prayers are meant to be a conduit between the worshiper and God. In fact, the use of formal language can cause worshipers to falsely believe that only this kind of language can be used when speaking to God and that normal human conversational language is inadequate. Again, let me show you what I mean.

Consider this prayer from a more traditional mainline church source, the Presbyterian Church (U.S.A.) *Book of Common Worship*:

> Eternal God,
> In whom we live and move and have our being:
> you have made us for yourself,
> so that our hearts are restless
> until they rest in you.
> Give us purity of heart and strength of purpose
> that no selfish passion may hinder us from knowing your will,
> no weakness keeps us from doing it,
> that in your light we might see light clearly,
> and in your service find perfect freedom;
> Through Jesus Christ our Lord,
> who lives and reigns with you and the Holy Spirit,
> one God now and forever. Amen.[4]

So what is wrong with this prayer? Nothing, from a traditional perspective. It uses wonderful, poetic language. It has a sense of depth and majesty. The issue is that for many people, it is not formative. It is tied to language from another era. It relies on nouns and prepositions, which tend to make speech feel ponderous, rather than verbs, which are lively and draw us in. It uses few emotive adjectives, and we live in an age in which expressive adjectives such as *awesome* are frequently used. It is humble language but not formative. See if this reconstruction of the above prayer seems more formative and able to connect the worshiper in prayer:

> Eternal God,
> We live in you. We move in you. We find ourselves in you.
> You created us, and you have a wonderful purpose for our lives.
> But our troubled souls toss and turn with anxiety,
> until we place ourselves calmly into your hands.
> Purify our tainted hearts
> and strengthen us so that we can find our purpose in life.
> Reduce the power of our overdriven egos, and give us humble
>   hearts,
> so that we can understand your purposes,
> follow your call,
> do your will,
> and thus become free to serve you;
> Through Jesus Christ, our Lord,
> in the power of the Holy Spirit,
> one God now and forever. Amen.

I certainly don't want to claim that this edit of a traditional prayer makes it the perfect formative prayer. But it does update the traditional liturgical language of prayer. To make it even more formative would mean using an oral style—a common, conversational tone, moving away from stilted language. Certainly, extemporaneous prayer can be stilted, so when I say "an oral style," I mean that we pray in a way that mimics the conversational nature of modern speaking.

Now, that said, there are times when using the more traditional language is more formative. I often use more traditional, scripted prayers when doing funerals for elderly people because I know they are the prayers traditional church members have grown up with, and they help the elderly connect better with God. Ultimately, the question is always, what is formative for the people whom we worship leaders are both leading in worship and trying to reach through worship? The point is to create prayers that act as a conduit, which means using language, and language constructions, that connect worshipers and God.

Music

Music is such a personal medium that it is difficult to specify how music can be formative. We are talking about an aspect of worship that touches parts of the mind and soul that sermons and prayers may not. Also, musical preferences vary among generations, regions, traditions, and individuals. What is formative to one group of people may be completely deformative to another. A hymn may open up one person spiritually while closing off another. Often, the power of a song depends on whether the song is one a person was raised with (some love hymns from their youth, others hate them), down- or up-tempo, in a major or minor key, played on the organ or more contemporary instruments such as guitars and drums, or written using traditional or contemporary language.

Those of us who select the music for worship must ask ourselves what kind of music is formative for the people worshiping with our congregation and those whom we are trying to reach. For example, if you have created a worship service targeting younger generations, then you will probably want to employ songs and anthems that are up-tempo, in a major key, and played on keyboards, guitars, and drums. If you are in a community of mostly retired people, then your worship will probably include songs played down-tempo, sometimes in a minor key, using an organ and classical instruments (although this stereotype will not be as accurate in ten to twenty years). Now, here comes the tricky part. If you are trying to create multigenerational worship that reaches across all ages, then you are going to want to hit all those themes.

The formative aspect of music also has to do with the themes of the songs themselves. Many songs are written in an informative rather than a formative style. Whether the lyrics are informative or formative has an impact on worshipers' experiences. I don't want to suggest that churches now only use songs written in a formative style, because that might cut out many wonderful hymns. But the fact is that many traditional and contemporary hymns are written in an informational, more abstract, third-person style. For example, look at the words of "A Mighty Fortress Is Our God":

A mighty fortress is our God, a bulwark never failing;
our helper he amid the flood of mortal ills prevailing.
For still our ancient foe doth seek to work us woe;
his craft and power are great, and armed with cruel hate,
on earth is not his equal.[5]

This hymn is one of my favorites, but it is written in an informational style. It can be very formative, because people who love it bring a formative spirit to singing it. Still, it is written in the third person, telling us about God but not necessarily connecting us with God. The same is true of many contemporary hymns. Take, for instance, a popular contemporary song such as "Mighty Is Our God." I encourage you to look up the lyrics by typing the title into your Web browser. You can find it on many sites. This is one of my favorite contemporary hymns, but, again, it is in the third person. The hymn is abstract, speaking about God but not necessarily connecting with God.

Contrast these with what may be considered a more formatively written hymn such as "Be Thou My Vision":

Be Thou my vision, O Lord of my heart;
Naught be all else to me, save that Thou art.
Thou my best thought, by day or by night,
Waking or sleeping, Thy presence my light.[6]

Or those of "Amazing Grace":

Amazing grace, how sweet the sound,
That saved a wretch like me.
I once was lost, but now am found,
Was blind, but now I see.[7]

In both cases the hymns are more formatively written, engaging the singer in a spiritual dialogue with God. In "Be Thou My Vision," the singer is offering a prayer to God, asking that God be his or her vision, allowing the singer to see through God's eyes. In "Amazing Grace," the hymn writer is engaging us in a personal story about how God's grace transformed him, and thus how grace transforms us. We can see how the pronouns in the songs engage the singer. In more formative songs, the pronouns used are *you*, *me*, and *I*. In informative songs, the pronoun is *he*.

Looking at a popular, more contemporary song, such as "Shout to the Lord," we can see the same principles at work. Again, I encourage you to look up the lyrics by typing the title into your computer's Web browser. This song—an intimate song expressing love and devotion between the worshiper and God—is one of the most universally popular contemporary songs, *and* it is written in the first person. I think these two facts are related.

The point of all this is not to sway worship leaders from using more informative hymns and songs, because even information can serve formation. It is to make us aware that songs written and sung in a more personal, formative way draw people in and may open them up to the workings of the Spirit.

AESTHETICS

How churches construct their worship spaces has a huge spiritual and formative impact on worshipers. Do the worship spaces invite people to experience and encounter the Holy? Again, this is a very subjective matter. What generation the worshiper is part of often determines the impact that a worship space will have on him or her. For instance, older worshipers, in general, are going to resonate with a more traditional space. They may prefer darker lighting, pews, pulpits, organs, and muted colors such as brown, beige, maroon, and dark shades of blue, green, or red. Depending on whether they come from a Reformed or a Catholic background, they might prefer walls with no art or decorations or walls filled with mosaics, carvings, banners, or other visuals. Nondenominational baby boomers often resonate with spaces that look and feel like auditoriums. They prefer brighter colors and lighting, individual fold-down seats, potted plants, simple podiums, rock-style musical instruments, and theatrical lighting. The Millennial generation seems to appreciate worship spaces that integrate both traditional and contemporary elements.

With all this said, the question churches need to ask is how well the aesthetics of our worship spaces help people encounter the Divine. At Calvin Presbyterian Church, we have spent a lot of time and effort thinking about this subject. We are determined to create a multigenerational congregation, so we have been very intentional about integrating elements that appeal to different generations. For instance, our sanctuary has a generally traditional aesthetic, with medium-hued oak pews, pulpit, communion railings and table, and baptismal font. A wooden Celtic cross is front and center. At the same time, and with a mind to the younger generations, we have bright lighting along with bright colors in banners, paraments, choir robes, and even my robes (the robes are part of the Presbyterian tradition). We have filled the sanctuary with color. We also have a sophisticated sound system and utilize PowerPoint projections when making announcements and to enhance sermons, such as running movie clips, showing pictures, and providing bullet-pointed outlines. Also, we have a large drama ministry that uses the sanctuary for plays, so we have theatrical lighting in the sanctuary, which can be set up for concerts and plays within thirty minutes to an hour. As a result, I have done many sermons in front of a set for *Godspell*, *Jesus Christ Superstar*, or *Joseph and the Amazing Technicolor Dreamcoat*. We adapt, but we also try very hard to create an aesthetic that opens people of all ages to an encounter with the Holy.

The point is not to push Calvin Church's aesthetic as an exemplar but to emphasize that churches need to be intentional about our aesthetic if we are to be formative. A question to ask about our worship spaces is whether they are designed to connect the Holy with those worshiping with the church now as well as those we are trying to reach. What is the experience of people as they enter the sanctuary? What is the experience of those we want to enter the sanctuary? The worship space has the power to act as a conduit between God and people. What are we doing to open that conduit wider?

What's the Point of Our Worship?

At Calvin, we frequently ask ourselves: How is God calling us to shape our worship in order to reach those God is seeking to embrace through worship? I think that the tragedy of too many mainline churches is that we aren't always very good at asking, with intentionality, what God is calling us to do through our worship. That doesn't mean church leaders don't grapple with worship. It's just that our motives can often be mixed. What drives the changes we make in worship?

I have talked to many pastors who have initiated change in worship because they personally didn't like something in the service. I can't tell you how many pastors I have come across who have told me about how they went to a new church, experienced something in worship that they really didn't like, changed it, and then were surprised by the backlash they experienced. The problem for many of them is that they didn't change the worship in order to make it more formative. They changed things so they would feel more comfortable. As worship leaders, we need to get out of the habit of asking, "What do I like or dislike?" and move to asking the question, "God, does this help people experience you?" Change the service if it has lost its power to help people encounter Christ, or if your church is trying to reach a new population. Don't change it to appease one person—in particular, the pastor. The question is always, how formative is the service to worshipers or potential worshipers?

Sometimes leaders make changes so that they can reach those outside the congregation—the unchurched. That's fine, but if we are trying to create a multigenerational congregation, is it wise to make changes only for those outside of our church without considering what helps those currently in our churches experience God? We have to keep both populations in mind.

Finally, if we keep things just as they are, are we only doing so to appease those already in the pews? Are we just giving in to customs and traditions that may be stifling the ability of younger worshipers to encounter God through our worship? The reason for keeping things as they are must correspond to our answer to the question, Does this way of worshiping allow people to connect with the Divine? Our worship must be grounded in a primary question: What kind of worship is God calling us to offer so that God can connect with those God is trying to reach?

Reflection Questions

1. As you reflect on the whole chapter, what concepts or points stood out for you and why?
2. Looking at your own church's worship service, to what extent would you say that the worship is either *intentionally spiritual* or *merely functional*?
3. Where do you see an *informative approach* being a dominant influence in your church's worship?
4. Where do you see a focus on a *formative approach* influencing your church's worship?
5. Reflect on what steps your church would have to take to create a more *formative* and *spiritual* approach in its worship services.

CHAPTER 4

Understanding Our Era

I HAD A CONVERSATION WITH A RETIRED PASTOR LAST YEAR, A PASTOR WHO had been very successful in ministry in his heyday. He had been the pastor of a church that during the 1960s and 1970s had grown from five hundred to fifteen hundred members in twelve years. Using the measuring stick that evangelical and mainline denominations normally use to gauge pastoral success, he would clearly be considered a success. I wondered what it was that allowed him to be successful, so we compared how worship was done then and now. His response confirmed my thoughts about modern worship, but at the same time made me a bit wistful for a bygone era. He said:

> We never had to think about the stuff churches need to think about now. We didn't have to think about whether to use contemporary or traditional hymns, technology, and PowerPoint. We didn't have to think about different generations and that stuff. We worried about three things: preaching, program, and pastoral care. If you did those three well enough, your church generally grew. Everyone did worship the same. You just played the same music year in and year out, sang the same hymns on a rotation, and everything took care of itself. Today, you guys have to worry about way too much. I'm glad I was a pastor when I was.

He confirmed what I already knew: being a pastor today is hard. Being a church today is hard. We live in an era very different from previous eras, a post-Christendom era in which worshiping weekly is not a given. Remnants of Christendom are still apparent in our culture. In the southeastern United States, a Christendom culture still thrives within the post-Christendom culture. For example, if you were to move to a city or town in Alabama, Georgia, North Carolina, or Texas, it would be typical for someone, upon meeting you, to ask what church you go to. If you say, none, they usually invite you to theirs. But the practice is waning in many places, including where I live, in Western Pennsylvania. Here, asking someone where she goes to church is considered rude or *nebby*—Pittsburghese for "getting into someone else's business."

Western Pennsylvania is somewhat Appalachian in culture, but it shares with other areas of the United States the reticence to talk about faith and church. This post-Christendom tendency to keep churchgoing out of daily conversation is increasingly common in the northeastern, as well as the northwestern, United States. What does it mean to be post-Christendom? It means that we live in an era in which churchgoing is no longer central to our cultural norms and mores. In fact, not going to church is increasingly becoming the norm. Increasingly, people who regularly go to church feel as though they are the misfits. Some of the teens of Calvin Church complain that they feel like they need to hide their church attendance from classmates at school because of the reactions they get.

The issue for us, as we try to create a church that connects people with the Holy, is that at present we are emerging from a transitional period between modernity and postmodernity. The eras have changed. We no longer live in an era in which the society shares generally one perspective on faith and life. In fact, we live in an individualized era, one in which people seek to create their own realities so that they can feel unique. The result is that perspectives on faith and religion commonly shared by our culture one hundred years ago are now consistently questioned. North America is quickly moving in the direction of Europe where less than 10 percent of the population attends worship even occasionally, let alone regularly. I don't think we will ever quite get to where Europe is, mainly because religion is so much a part of the fabric of U.S. culture, and because religions in the United States are much more adept at adapting to cultural changes. But we are becoming less religious.

This transition from the modern to the postmodern era is embodied in the different generations. Some generational researchers have identified the Millennial generation, the generation born between 1984 and 2004, as the first postmodern generation, while others suggest Generation X may be the first born into this new era. The impact of this shift is that the church contends with not only normal generational differences but also the fact that these generations are rooted in different eras.

The impact on worship is that if we are to offer multigenerational worship, we must appeal to at least three, if not four, distinct generational cohorts. Each one has its own desires, and they do not mix all that well. One of the several well-known church researchers whose work I follow (I am sorry to say, I do not remember which one) was fond of saying, "If you want your church to grow, it's better to start a church targeting one or two generations. One of the most difficult tasks of all is to turn around a traditional church in decline." He has a point. Targeting one generation is much easier than trying to reach several. Creating a baby boomer church, a Generation X church, or a Millennial generation church is easier than creating one that hits all of them. In fact, one of the problems of the mainline church is that we tend to target only one generation—one that is now between ages 65 and 85, a generation that is waning.

Churches face these basic questions regarding worship and the era we are in: first, how do we reach out to people rooted in both modern and postmodern perspectives? And second, how do church leaders help the church transition to what will increasingly become a postmodern culture? Much of the worship conflict in churches has to do with people rooted in one era reacting against attempts to reach someone rooted in another era. In this chapter we will explore the nature of the modern and postmodern eras and discuss how to create a multigenerational experience that spans these eras.

The Modern to Postmodern Transition

For much of my adult life I have heard the terms *premodern, modern,* and *postmodern* bandied about in conversations, especially among people fascinated with theology and philosophy. The problem I always have had is that I never understood what they were talking about. People would try to describe postmodernism using terms such as *deconstructionism*, but I still didn't know what it meant to be postmodern other than to be against all basic philosophical and theological propositions. To my uninformed mind, to be postmodern was to be feminist or liberationist, and I kept my distance from them because they seemed like positions staked out because of what they stood against—patriarchy and oppression—rather than what they stood for. My question back then was, How do churches create a worship experience based on deconstruction?

The writings of an interesting man named Ken Wilber helped me begin to understand the differences between the eras as well as what era I identify with. Wilber is not your normal philosopher. He does not have a full-time teaching position, but he has devoted his life to reading and studying a myriad of disciplines, while periodically producing books that integrate different perspectives. In this approach, he is completely postmodern, as you will see in bit. His writings integrate disparate fields of philosophy, theology, spirituality, psychology, economics, physics, biology, and other sciences. His book *The Marriage of the Sense and Soul* is what finally helped me understand the term *postmodern*.[1]

To understand what it means to be postmodern, it helps to start with an understanding of the premodern perspective. Throughout this whole discussion, my interest is in helping church leaders gain a clearer understanding of these three great eras of Western civilization and how they influence worship practices. I am not interested in engaging in a nuanced philosophical or theological discussion of the different eras, so I will be speaking in broad terms. I am seeking to define each era simply and clearly rather than specifically and definitively. My definitions will have a lot to be desired philosophically and theologically, but they will help us understand how worship has been transformed over the past two thousand years.

Premodernity in the Western world extended over a one-thousand-year period lasting roughly from the time Christianity was established as the state religion of the Roman Empire in AD 326, until the Renaissance, which began around the fourteenth century and extended into the seventeenth century. According to Wilber, during this period the three great emphases of life—art, morals, and science—were dominated by one perspective: the church's.[2] The Western world had only one perspective on truth, and it was whatever the Roman Catholic Church said it was. Therefore, all art, philosophy, and science had to correspond to the Church's beliefs. If you look at pre-Renaissance art, philosophy, and science, all of them focused on preconceived truths handed down from the Church. Thus, this period didn't experience much development in the way of science, which requires independent thinking and research. The rigidity of the premodern perspective eventually led to conflict whenever independent-minded thinkers broke from Church doctrine. For instance, as the premodern period gave way to the modern one, conflict ensued when Galileo used telescopic observations to support the theories of Copernicus that said the earth revolved around the sun, which conflicted with the Church's view that the sun revolved around the earth. Galileo's problem was that by offering objective, modernist truth, he was vying with premodern truth, which states that the only truth is the Church's truth.

Galileo lived in a period of transition and transformation much like ours today. Beginning with the Renaissance and growing through the Age of Enlightenment (beginning in the mid-seventeenth century), other truth perspectives began to compete with the church's truth. He was developing his theories during the advent of modernity. The modern period was marked by what Wilber calls the *differentiation of the cultural value spheres*, meaning that there was a "differentiation of art, morals, and science. Where previously these spheres tended to be fused, modernity differentiated them and let each proceed at its own pace with its own dignity, using its own tools, following its own discoveries, unencumbered by intrusions from the other spheres."[3] To reframe what Wilber wrote more succinctly, we can say that despite the human desire to hold onto only one truth, that being *religious* truth, humans were discovering other truth perspectives in the world. People were starting to ascertain truths that competed with religious truth—artistic truth, philosophical truth, and scientific truth. The result is that the biologist could say, "There is only a biological truth in the world that we should seek." The physicist could say, "There is only a physical truth in the world that we should seek." The artist could say, "There is only an artistic truth in the world that we should seek."

As the Renaissance gave way to the Enlightenment, proponents of these different fields of truth began to compete with one another over what constituted truth. Now advocates of each field saw themselves as purveyors of the *true* truth. You can see vestiges of this on college campuses, where each discipline treats its own perspective as the one, true perspective. I remember experiencing this in college. Those majoring in the "hard" sciences—biology, chemistry, physics—looked down on us who majored in the "social" sciences—psychology, sociology, and anthropology. We all sort of looked down on the philosophy and religion majors, because they didn't use any science at all. We all had our own truth perspectives, and we knew ours was the right one. Modernity, in many ways, has been an attempt to find that one true truth perspective while simultaneously dismissing others. Exemplifying this idea is a quote from the famed economist, John Maynard Keynes, who once said, "The ideas of economists and political philosophers, both when they are right and when they are wrong, are more powerful than is commonly understood. Indeed the world is ruled by little else."[4] Apparently for him, the only *true* perspectives are economic and political.

The fragmentation of truth into competing spheres is what made the Reformation possible. The Reformers broke down the Roman Catholic Church's monopoly on religious truth by encouraging people to read Scripture for themselves. Basing their respective approaches on their reading of Scripture, each new Christian sect proclaimed itself to have the truth. At first the different sects looked for ways to dialogue with one another, but being true modernists, they eventually saw one another as competing for the one "true" truth, and so each denigrated the others. The fact that all Protestant denominations emerged in the midst of the modern period has resulted in their tendency to fight modernist theological battles with one another over truth—a five-hundred-year battle. The battles aren't merely between denominations. Modernist truth battles are waged between religious ideological movements. Both the fundamentalist and the evangelical movements have been attempts to create systems of truth, as have the progressive Christian movements emphasizing social justice. Each group finds ways to proclaim itself the bearer of the truth, while to some degree denigrating those who promote alternate beliefs.

The postmodern era began as the nineteenth century gave way to the twentieth, and while we at the beginning of the twenty-first century are technically in the postmodern era, we are also experiencing it as a transition between the modern and postmodern periods. Who started the postmodern era is impossible to say. It may have started with the Romantics of nineteenth-century music (such as Schubert, Schumann, Chopin, and Wagner) and literature (such as Keats, Shelley, and Poe), or the Transcendentalists (such as Thoreau and Emerson). The Romanticists were reacting to the emphasis on intellectual logic and rationalization that was gaining popularity during the Age of Enlightenment. They were trying to emphasize *emotional experience* as being important to life. In effect, they were offering an alternative perspective to the intellectualization and mechanization of life that had become so common in an age of industrialization. The point is that they offered other viewpoints, questioning any stance claimed as *the* truth. In fact, as postmodernism has grown, it has led to the challenging of any individual or group who presents only one perspective as the truth.

For example, the art of Pablo Picasso often baffles the modernist mind because he was trying to paint pictures from many different perspectives at once. Instead of following the pattern of traditional paintings, which offer one perspective, he might paint a portrait that integrated three perspectives—a woman looking forward, sideways, and up, all at the same time. The advent of quantum theory in physics at the end of the nineteenth century, introduced by Albert Einstein (among others), allowed scientists to question any one scientific truth perspective. An example of this is the discovery that light exhibits the characteristics of both a collection of particles and a wave. Whether a researcher observes light as particles or as waves all depends on the observer's perspective, for both perspectives are true, even if they are contradictory.

Postmodernity has often been defined more as the *rejection* of truth rather than as the *projection* of truth.[5] Often it is said that the postmodern approach is an attempt to undermine and *deconstruct* any claims of objective or absolute truth. If biological science claims to offer truth, the postmodern biologist will tear down and deconstruct assumptions about biological truth. The same can be said of a postmodern approach to psychology, politics, theology, spirituality, physics, art, economics, medicine, or anything else. For example, all the following could be deconstructionist, postmodern statements:

- All Western medicine is false because it considers the body only as a machine.
- Western religion and politics are riddled with patriarchal systems that need to be torn down.
- Capitalism is the problem. It oppresses the poor. So it must be torn down, and anything that rises will be better.

Each of these statements contains some sort of truth, but each mainly pulls down a belief system rather than promoting an alternative. Thus, many see the postmodern movement as a cynical, deconstructionist movement rather than as one that promotes a positive point of view.

Personally, I believe the deconstructionist perspective is a limited one, and that it arose because postmodernity has had a hard time defining itself. It is easier to criticize a truth perspective than to offer an alternative one. In recent years the postmodern perspective has begun to offer more coherent belief systems based on interpretation—based on the recognition that our perception of truth changes depending on how we interpret the world. In other words, it recognizes the importance and possibility of interpreting truth in light of a variety of perspectives. The postmodernist appreciates that some sort of absolute truth may exist, but we humans have a very hard time ascertaining it because our ability to grasp and understand is limited.

Deconstructionists tear down the assertions of those who claim to have grasped absolute truth. They do what my younger brother used to say to me whenever I would say that something was a fact: "How do you know? You're not God!" Whenever he would say this, it would infuriate me. But at some level, he was right. How can we know anything for sure? Aren't we all just limited by our perspectives?

A more positive postmodern approach agrees that there may be absolute truth, but it can only be ascertained as we approach it from different perspectives. So a postmodern approach embraces *integration*. It embraces an approach that is willing to look at an ideology, belief system, or any subject matter from a variety of perspectives. For instance, if we are dealing with a psychological problem—say, a person suffering from depression—we look at the person's difficulties not only from a psychological perspective but also from a biological one (How might the person's diet, physical condition, and brain chemistry and structure contribute to the depression?); an economic one (How might the person's financial situation be contributing to the depression?); a historical one (How does this person's past contribute to the depression?); and a spiritual one (How does this person's spirituality, or lack of spirituality, contribute to the depression?). The result is an integrated perspective. Often problems become resolved by approaching a situation from a series of fresh perspectives. That's being postmodern.

We in the early twenty-first century have entered the postmodern age. We can see examples of the search for a variety of perspectives reflected in much of contemporary film. For example, the 1999 science-fiction film *The Matrix* was one of the first clearly postmodern films. It offered a new perspective on reality by revealing that what the main character, Neo, thought was reality turned out to be the construction of a massive computer that he, along with everyone else in the world, was linked into. Even the fight scenes were visually postmodern. As a fight progressed, the characters would be frozen in space as our perspective swung around and showed the fight from a 360-degree perspective. We see postmodernism reflected in musicals such as *Into the Woods* (1986) and *Wicked* (2003). *Into the Woods* shows what happened to various characters from Grimm's fairly tales after the stories ended. Not all turned out well. *Wicked* is the story of *The Wizard of Oz* told from the Wicked Witch of the West's perspective. She turned out to be good and was only appearing to be bad so that she could eventually be freed to live life with her true love. Both of these are postmodern because they offer new perspectives on accepted truths—that Grimm's creatures all lived "happily ever after" and that the characters in *The Wizard of Oz* were good and evil as portrayed. These plays have a lot in common with Picasso and Einstein, both of whom offered windows on new perspectives.

What Is the "Right" Way to Worship?

So, let's bring this back to worship. What does postmodernity have to do with modern worship? A lot. Christian worship has always reflected its era. Premodern worship was pretty straightforward. It was whatever the Church said it was. So, for approximately eleven hundred years in Europe, very little changed in worship. Even today in the Roman Catholic Church, worship is remarkably consistent in churches the world over. Why? Because the Church hierarchy in Rome, or in each country, sets the order of worship as well as provides the prayers. There is not much variety of worship between regions and countries. The Roman Catholic tradition is rooted in premodernism, which has created problems for the Church as it has dealt, first of all, with members who were captivated by the modern movement, and now by those captured by the postmodern movement.

The modernist movement, marked by competing truth claims, allowed for diversity in worship among different denominations. Instead of only one way to worship (the Roman Catholic way), modernists offered new theories of worship, each one claiming that it was the right way of worshiping. So we have Calvinist worship and Zwinglian worship (both competing within the Reformed tradition), Lutheran worship, Anabaptist worship, Quaker worship, Anglican worship, and now contemporary worship. These respective practices of worship arose out of their respective doctrinal belief systems. Thus, each tradition has had its own orthodoxy (right doctrinal beliefs) that has resulted in its own orthopraxy (right religious practices). Many of the worship battles today are between modernist churchgoers who believe that there is really only one right way to worship—a way that emerges out of the one right theological system.

A postmodern approach to worship basically says that there isn't one right way to worship. Instead, there are all sorts of viable approaches. For example, the Anglican practice can be wonderful because of its emphasis on liturgy and sacraments, but so can the Quaker practice with its emphasis on silence and centering. Each offers a different experience that connects the worshiper with God. Thus, a postmodern approach to worship would be an integrative approach, which is what I have been advocating in this book. Clearly, I am postmodern, but in a positive, constructionist way, not in a cynical, deconstructionist way. I believe that we have already passed into a new period of postmodernism—one defined by an appreciation of different perspectives, rather than by the deconstruction of prior perspectives. We live in a culture that constantly advocates diversity—diversity of race, ethnicity, gender, culture, political beliefs, and sexual orientation. If we are trying to reach postmodern people in our churches, then approaching them in a postmodern way through worship is crucial.

Postmodern worship is integrative worship, integrating different musical styles, rituals, and aesthetics. For example, at Calvin Presbyterian Church we are intentional about incorporating classical, gospel, contemporary, rhythm and blues, and even pop music into our worship. We integrate rituals gleaned from Presbyterian, Lutheran, Roman Catholic, evangelical, Episcopal, contemporary, emergent, and other traditions. We also may introduce practices from nonChristian faiths, although that is much rarer.

The battles that so many churches often engage in while transforming worship, so-called "worship wars," arise either because churches are offering competing modernist approaches (traditional and contemporary) or because churches are in transition from a modernist to a postmodernist approach. On the one hand, proponents of both traditional and contemporary worship claim to offer the right kind of worship. On the other hand, conflict between traditional and integrative worship, or between contemporary and emergent worship (many advocates of contemporary worship bemoan the emergent movement), is a conflict between modernists, who say there is only one right way (orthopraxy), and postmodernists, who advocate an integration of worship styles (polypraxy).

The competing pull of traditional worship styles and emerging possibilities has resulted in denominations finding themselves between two worlds, with their theology caught in one era and their worship in another. For instance, among mainline churches, our *theology* is becoming increasingly postmodern as we become open to and integrate different theological perspectives. In our *worship*, however, we operate in the modernist perspective, which says there is only one right way to worship, one that entails pastors wearing robes (black is preferable), prayers being written and spoken by experts, music being classical and traditional (often played on the organ), and sanctuaries maintaining a traditional aesthetic. Meanwhile, the evangelical movement's *theology* is firmly rooted in the modernist perspective, advocating *one* way of reading Scripture, *one* way of understanding Christianity, and *one* way of "being saved," while their *worship* becomes thoroughly postmodern, welcoming any practice as long as it reaches the seeker and the unchurched.

I need to clarify something here. Earlier I said contemporary worship is a modernist form of worship. However, I believe that it is no longer beholden to the modernist era. Only the more traditional evangelical churches remain steadfastly contemporary. Over the past ten years, many established evangelical churches have become willing to try and experiment with anything, as long as it reaches seekers.

The emergent movement is much more of a postmodern movement. Most emergent churches offer a certain perspective on interpreting and understanding the Bible, but they mostly refuse to get caught up in the theological battles over women's ordination, abortion, homosexuality, salvation, and other issues that tend to be divisive. Instead, they tend to be more intentional about integrating different perspectives. Their worship is also postmodern in the sense that it integrates ancient, traditional, contemporary, and idiosyncratic practices.

What I am advocating as a renewed vision for the mainline church is not just a mainline version of the emergent movement. I am advocating a worship style that begins to match our theological diversity. The mainline church has been grappling with a growing diversity of theological thought along many lines, such as the understanding of who Jesus Christ was and is, what the Trinity means, what it means to be a Christian, and the ever-perplexing issue of homosexuality and ordination. Mainline theology is becoming much less monolithic and much more open to different perspectives on previously held beliefs, but this transition has been neither smooth nor easy. This growing diversity has caused a tremendous amount of conflict within our denominations.

The mainline church is presently grappling to integrate insights not only from biblical scholarship but also from modern psychology, sociology, anthropology, biology, economics, and other fields. Many of the internal tensions we experience are between those who believe that the only locus of truth is Scripture and those who believe that, while we need to begin with Scripture, we should also integrate insights and discoveries from other fields. These are modernist versus postmodernist tensions. These tensions are about theological matters, but they are especially evident in worship matters. We are caught in a tension about whether worship should adhere only to one "right" tradition or integrate a variety of traditions. The challenge for us is that our culture is increasingly becoming postmodern, so to stake out a modernist position affects our ability as a church to reach beyond our present congregations to those who are unchurched or "dechurched"—that is, those who have left a church because of dissatisfaction.

How Do We Know What's Right in a Postmodern World?

One of the biggest issues facing mainline churches as we try to create worship in an increasingly postmodern culture is deciding how to determine what is right to do. The problem with postmodernism is relativity—the idea that everything is relative and so nothing is absolutely right. This philosophy is, ahem . . . , relatively speaking, rooted in Einstein's special theory of relativity— $E=MC^2$—which gave rise to his general theory of relativity. This is a physics theory that has to do with the impact of velocity on mass and energy.

The basic theory, which is now an accepted fact, is that energy is always a reflection of an object's mass and velocity, and vice versa. In other words, energy (E) is not a constant, but it is determined by the weight of an object (M) multiplied by the square of how fast it is moving (C). Also, it means that mass shifts, depending on how fast it is moving and on the energy exerted in moving it.

This all has implications, for example, on time, making the passage of time relative. Thus, if we are moving slowly through the universe on a planet that has a very heavy mass, and therefore has a strong gravity, we will move more quickly through time than if we are on a spaceship that has very little gravity and is moving very quickly. Thus, time is relative to the speed at which we are moving and the gravitational pull we are under.

Postmodernism has taken this theory of physics and applied it to life. It is one reason that Einstein could legitimately be said to be one of the progenitors of postmodern theory, even if he would have been appalled at the thought. Despite developing the theory of relativity, he was a Newtonian physicist at heart, which means that he believed that eventually someone would come along to show how what seemed relative was really just the intersection of fixed principles. Einstein was very uncomfortable with the idea of unpredictability. He was further bothered by another theory of his that many also use to support their postmodern theory of relativity[6]—his observation of *quanta*, the fact that light could be observed as both a wave and a packet of particles, and that the observer's perspective determines what is observed. While this is not a theory under his general theory of relativity, many postmodernists have used it to underpin the postmodern theory of relativity.

At its extreme, postmodernism says that everything is relative and that nothing is certain. When postmodernists say this, they aren't being truthful, since some things are actually certain. But their point is that the principles and concepts of life are much less certain than we once thought and that often things are relative to our perspective. For instance, to say that there is only one way to worship depends on your perspective. As a Roman Catholic I might be able to agree with that, but as a nonChristian I could not.

So, back to the original question: How do mainline churches determine what's right to do in our worship? The easiest thing to do is to pick a traditional worship order and say it's right, or to just do whatever we want and say that it's right. Leonard Sweet, a theologian who has written extensively on how the church needs to change to meet the future, has been very helpful in suggesting ways to cut through the confusion, although those looking for certainty will not find him helpful. Sweet suggests that we can conceive of present-day congregations as being like ships exploring the oceans in search of the New World, a world in which there are no maps. As a result, church leaders "need navigational skills that can take them from where they find themselves or where God has placed them to where God is calling them to go."[7] To navigate through these seas of seeming relativity, through the confusion of our times that holds no truths to be true, people need to hold on to that which is certain.

For the navigator, certainty is found in a compass and the North Star. For Sweet, our compass is the Bible.[8] And the North Star is Christ.[9] Many people think that their tradition is the constant, but as I said in previous chapters, traditions change. Sweet says that tradition is like an anchor.[10] Anchors are good when ships are in harbors, when people are in stable times, but they can become dangerous when the winds shift and storms assault us. In other words, when we go through rapidly changing times, being stuck rigidly in a tradition can actually harm us, much in the same way that a ship at anchor in a harbor during a hurricane is in much more danger than a ship out at sea. Both places are dangerous, but at least when sailors are at sea, they can ride out the storm and shift positions to put them in a safer place. In a harbor, they are stuck in place, and the rocks are much closer and pose a much greater risk.

So, once again, how do we know what's right? By prayerfully seeking Christ's guidance as we consider changes and by ensuring that whatever we do is consonant with Scripture. I have said this very simply, but you already know that this is not simple. We disagree over what the Bible says and what Christ may be calling us to. I suppose it is no different from confusion over how a compass works and where the North Star is. To follow the North Star, you have to know where to look. To follow Christ in prayer, you have to know how to pray in a way that is sensitive to Christ's leadings. There is always the danger that someone will claim to be prayerful and then mislead us, in the same way that when in the midst of people who are ignorant of where the North Star is, anyone can say confidently that any star is the North Star.

The North Star is easy to find for those who know where it is. Just find the Big Dipper, and then follow the imaginary line from the front lip of the dipper upwards to the next visible star, the first star in the handle of the Little Dipper. Something similar can be said of seeking Christ's will in worship. We might say that finding Christ's will is relatively easy for those who know how to find it. The problem is that too few churches and their leaders ask the question, What kind of worship does Christ call us to offer? Fewer listen for an answer.

What needs to be clear here is that, just as not every star is the North Star, not every possibility is Christ's calling—that is, to be postmodern doesn't mean to see every possibility as relative. Being postmodern means to understand that the ability to ascertain truth and what God wants is limited and that the more churches and worship leaders are able to broaden their perspectives on what can be done in worship, the more they will be able to discern what God wants. When it comes to worship, that means seeking to create worship that offers a variety of perspectives so that they can reach people who are in different places musically, aesthetically, theologically, and spiritually. Still, they have to start with a foundational perspective and work from there.

The foundational perspective of any Christian worship has to be Scripture and Christ, or more specifically, the Trinity. The temptation for many churches, in their desire to reach postmodern generations, is to do anything to reach them. That may mean eschewing a Christian foundation for one that assimilates where the culture is spiritually or materially. The death in July 2009 of "Reverend Ike," Rev. Frederick J. Eikerenkoetter II, reminded me of how easy it is to morph Christian beliefs into cultural beliefs.

Reverend Ike was one of the first proponents of what has come to be known as the prosperity gospel. He was pastor of the United Church Science of Living Institute in New York City, a church that he founded based on his own Christian principles. He was a prominent televangelist during the 1970s, promoting a gospel that said that the Bible got it wrong—God wanted us to be wealthy. As his obituary quotes him as saying: "If it's that difficult for a rich man to get into heaven," he said, riffing on a verse from the Book of Matthew, "think how terrible it must be for a poor man to get in. He doesn't even have a bribe for the gatekeeper."[11] Reverend Ike amassed millions of dollars throughout his life by preaching that God wants us to have prosperity and to be rich. Like many other prosperity gospel preachers after him, who preach that the Gospels teach that God wants us to be successful and wealthy, using the parable of the talents as his guide, Reverend Ike inspired thousands to pursue wealth as a pathway to God. The problem is that he subsumed Scripture and the teachings of Christ under the message of capitalism. To offer this perspective on Christian truth is not postmodern. It is disingenuous.

To be grounded in Scripture and the Trinity is to be grounded in an attempt to preach, teach, and reflect what Scripture says, aided by our prayerful seeking of Christ's will, in a way that has integrity to the gospel while seeking ways to articulate it to an ever-changing culture.

Postmodern Worship

Whether we are ready or not, Western culture has entered the postmodern era. Modern technology, especially the Internet with its vast reserves of information, is speeding us there. We are faced with a dilemma in the modern church: move forward or possibly die. Churches that cling to traditional forms of worship, whether theologically, spiritually, homiletically, musically, or aesthetically, will slowly die. They are like people standing in a river, arms stretched forward, trying to hold back the current. They can rage against the waters, but they won't hold them back. So, what do we do to roll with the current?

Preaching from Multiple Perspectives

One of the primary differences between postmodern and modern movements has to do with how pastors preach. Preaching from a modernist perspective is a matter of presenting "the truth" to others and then explaining how belief in that truth saves us or otherwise affects us. Much traditional preaching, whether mainline or evangelical, is modernist—that is, it offers one perspective. It presents biblical and Christian truth as a given and then expects tacit agreement from worshipers. (To be traditional doesn't necessarily mean being modernist, but since traditional preaching was developed during the modernist era, they are fairly close to being the same thing.)

Nothing is really wrong with modernist preaching as long as the worshipers already share perspectives with the pastors. For much of American history worshipers generally have. Since the majority of people were born and buried in the same denominational tradition, they were generally exposed to one religious truth—the denomination's. That situation no longer exists. Increasingly, pastors are preaching to congregations that are ideologically, theologically, and denominationally diverse.

Look at your own congregation. What percentage of worshipers were born in your church or even your own denomination? I look at Calvin Presbyterian Church, and our members have very diverse roots. About 30 percent are former Roman Catholics. About 25 percent grew up Presbyterian. The rest come from Anglican, Baptist, Christian and Missionary Alliance, Christian Scientist, Disciples of Christ, Dutch Reformed, Episcopalian, Lutheran, Methodist, nondenominational, New Age, and unchurched roots. Each Sunday I preach is a challenge because I can't just assume that everyone is on the same wavelength. Some may be familiar with Scripture, but many aren't. Some come from churches that stress the sacraments over Scripture, others from churches that stress Scripture over sacraments. Some are very comfortable with Christian language, while others are deeply ensconced in New Age or Eastern religious language. There are no givens. So to preach to all worshipers, I have to be willing to engage them from a variety of perspectives, which intentionally broadens each person's perspective.

How do preachers engage people where they are while also broadening them? It starts with me being very clear about what my foundation is while also working to understand theirs. As a postmodern preacher, I can't just be traditionally Presbyterian and Reformed. I need to understand the progressive perspective. I need to understand the evangelical perspective. I need to understand a New Age perspective.

I also can't preach in a way that denigrates their positions while emphasizing my own. My goal is to broaden their perspectives so that they can see the same truth I see. To expand their view, I have to create a bridge between their perspectives and mine. If I start by discounting their perspectives, then I will be tuned out. So, I have to try to use their language, if I can.

Preaching from a variety of perspectives is very similar to what Jesus did. Jesus translated his theology into the language of his listeners. They were mostly shepherds and farmers, so he used agrarian metaphors in his parables. In a similar way, Paul preached and taught in a diverse culture, speaking to both Jews and Gentiles. He was forced to walk a tricky balance, which is why Paul can be difficult for us to read. He had to use language that was both Jewish and Gentile, while moving folks of his time to an alternative perspective—one emphasizing how Christ transforms our minds, hearts, and souls; how grace is at work in our lives; and how the Spirit is leading us in life.

The Roman Empire, prior to the establishment of Christianity as the state religion between AD 326 and 350, was very similar to our postmodern culture. Religion in the Roman Empire was a mishmash of different beliefs. Some believed in the Greek gods. Some shared a Persian faith emphasizing astrology and the influence of the stars. Some had a Jewish faith. Some, such as the

Epicurians, the Stoics, the Aristotelians, and the Neoplatonists, followed Greek and Roman philosophies. Christianity vied for attention in a diverse world of religious beliefs. As Christianity progressed, it flourished precisely because it was able to integrate different perspectives. Chapter 2 explored this, when discussing St. Patrick's success. Christianity grew because it could expand people's perspectives to include a Christian one.

For preaching, it isn't just a matter of using metaphors from the surrounding culture. It's also a matter of being aware of the language and beliefs of people coming from mainline Protestant, Roman Catholic, evangelical, and New Age perspectives. So how do we preach in a diverse way? I think the simplest way is to acknowledge other perspectives and then explain the Christian perspective on the issue. For example, if I were trying to make the case for Christian worship in a sermon, I might say something to this effect:

> You know, some Christians say that unless you go to church every Sunday, you are destined to go to hell. They have a point, which is that if we aren't worshiping on a regular basis, we lose contact with God. Meanwhile, others who have walked away from church will tell you that the church is full of hypocrites and that you don't need the church to discover God in your life. They have a point, too. They recognize that we all have a responsibility to nourish a personal spirituality, one that isn't taken care of when we go to church every Sunday because we are scared of going to hell.
>
> I hear both sides, and I think both have valid points, but I think both miss where God can be found. The church isn't here to get you into heaven; the church is here to help you experience heaven in your life. Whether God accepts you or me into heaven isn't a matter of how many worship services we attend. God gets to choose based on whatever criteria God uses. But I also know that regular worship opens us to God and connects us with God in ways that we can't do alone. So many who have walked away from the church have also shut themselves off from experiencing heaven—the eternal—in this life by ignoring the need to create a discipline with others that includes prayer, praising God,

and listening for God. Perhaps we can do that on our own, but who does? Regular worship opens us to the Divine in ways that obligatory worship or the solitary walk cannot.

If you look at what I have done, I have identified two perspectives, and then offered an alternative to both. I didn't necessarily denigrate the other two perspectives as much as I suggested another way of looking at it that integrated the other two. I didn't come out and say that the other two were wrong. I only said they were limited. The point is that if we are going to help postmodern Christians become open to Christian faith, we have to realize that asserting only one truth, one that obliterates their truth, is a losing proposition. When most people are told that their ideas are wrong, they become defensive and resistant. If we offer an alternative, while validating something of their ideas, we gain the possibility of opening them to another perspective.

Again, I believe this is something that Jesus did. Jesus did obliterate the truth of some people, but it was generally those who were rigidly religious. He was much gentler with those of a different mindset. You can find an example in the parable of the good Samaritan (Luke 10:25–37). Jesus was responding to a testing question from a young lawyer, a man immersed in Jewish law. Jesus answered in a biblical way, validating the first commandment, but then went on in the telling of the parable to suggest an alternative perspective—that the person truly following the commandment was someone considered unrighteous by Jewish religious authorities. Jesus validated the command to love God and others, but then he broadened his listeners' perspectives by suggesting that the righteously religious people—the priest and the Levite—failed to follow the law, while the sinful person, the Samaritan, succeeded. That, to me, is a postmodern parable.

A large part of postmodern preaching is validating other perspectives as much as possible, recognizing that some perspectives can't be validated while showing how the Christian perspective is a fuller revelation rather than the "right" revelation. To start with a position that "I'm right, all others are wrong" is to turn off those who already are tempted to see Christians as intolerant, bigoted, and narrow-minded.

Integration of Various Ages, Eras, and Traditions

In many ways postmodernism also attempts to integrate perspectives from different ages and eras. Looking at the emergent church movement, a postmodern movement, we see it purposefully integrates elements from different ages. While every emergent church is different, this integration is consistent. For instance, an emergent church may have a praise band, but it often is one that plays traditional hymns in a contemporary meter. They may use PowerPoint, but often they project images such as ancient Celtic crosses, stained-glass windows from cathedrals, and ancient Christian ruins. They may also project nature scenes, people holding hands, or candles. Darker lighting, candles, and regular celebration of sacraments are often features. In some, pastors dress casually but wrapped in a traditional Jewish prayer shawl. Plenty of contemporary elements are used, too. The point is that they integrate elements from every age of Christianity.

The emergent movement can serve as a guide for mainline churches. To be postmodern means to recognize the value of the traditional, while also being open to instilling new rituals and practices. Many churches today choose between traditional and contemporary, offering a traditional service and a contemporary service. To me that seems like a modernist compromise, choosing between two disparate truths—traditional worship is the "right" form versus contemporary worship is the "right" form.

As we have explored before, one alternative to choosing one or the other form of worship is an approach that intentionally integrates ancient, classical, modern, and contemporary elements. There is no one right way to bring these elements together, only what is right for particular congregations. This is where Leonard Sweet's metaphor about being focused on the Christ, the North Star, is helpful. When it comes to integrating different elements, worship leaders need to be immersed in prayer, asking how Christ is calling us to minister to those already in the churches' pews as well as to those who aren't.

This prayer is difficult because we get in our own way. For the most part, established churches tend to ignore prayer and either follow what they have always done or implement whatever strategies they can to get people to attend. The prayerful, post-modern way is to try to understand the community and to integrate different elements by being sensitive to where people are, what they need, and what the congregation is called to do as a community. It means asking pastoral staff, worship leaders, committee members, and board members to engage in a prayerful program that seeks an answer to the question, "What will help these people best experience and encounter the Holy in worship?"

What Does This All Mean?

The fact that we in the West are in a period of cultural transition between the modern and postmodern eras means that there are no longer any hard-and-fast rules, except in the minds of those who create conflict over our choices. The conflict between these ages was demonstrated a number of years ago by two members of Calvin Presbyterian who eventually left to join other churches. For about a year, both of these members would occasionally come out of worship, shake my hand, and complain about worship.

The first was an elderly man in his early eighties who would complain that we weren't playing the organ enough. He would say that the organ was God's instrument, and if we weren't playing the organ, we weren't doing worship right. The fact is that for a number of years we have been moving away from the organ for both practical and postmodern reasons. The practical reason is that despite getting the organ tuned four times a year, our organ has been slowly deteriorating. It slips in and out of tune depending on temperature and humidity. Also, our musicians have diverse backgrounds ranging from classical to jazz to rock and are wonderful on piano and keyboards. We wanted to give them the freedom to diversify the sound. The postmodern reason is that we have been attempting to diversify the music in worship. Many of the songs and hymns we include in our services aren't appropriate for the organ.

So, how did I respond to the man? I told him that the organ is part of the mix of music we play, but that we are trying to use more than just an organ.

Meanwhile, a few minutes later, a woman in her thirties would come through the line and shake my hand. Often she would say to me, "We should be doing all contemporary worship. Contemporary worship is the wave of the future." I would tell her that other waves are coming and that I thought contemporary worship was on the wane. "Besides, we aren't just trying to reach younger people but people of all generations."

Neither answer satisfied either person, mainly because each one saw his or her preferred worship style as preeminent. They left me frustrated until I came to a realization: we are in a period of transition. The new rules for worship are just being formed right now, while the old rules for worship are either slowly fading or being transformed.

This means that we who are trying to create worship in this era have to proceed patiently. Generations tied to one form of worship are slowly dying away, while generations ready for another form are only slowly coming to the fore. We need to lead our churches through a transition, but at the same time do it in a way that includes rather than excludes people of different perspectives.

We face a difficult task.

Reflection Questions

1. As you reflect on the whole chapter, what concepts or points stood out for you and why?
2. In terms of it being *premodern, modern,* or *postmodern,* where do you see your church's worship?
3. To what extent is your church open to *integrative worship,* and to what extent is it mired in a traditional versus contemporary approach?
4. Recognizing that the culture around us is rapidly becoming more *postmodern* in its thinking, what steps could your church take in worship to reach out to the culture?

Chapter 5

Integrated Worship

For a long time now, I have been fascinated with how structure influences process. Far too often, we in the religious sphere don't pay attention to how important proper structure is for creating healthy churches. Like many other lessons, I have learned about the importance of structure from athletics. Although I can hardly call myself an athlete anymore, especially with an arthritic right knee that doesn't let me do much more than walk, in my youth through young adulthood, I played soccer, ice hockey, lacrosse, racquetball, track and field—and I learned a lot from all of them. I have also been a lifelong fan of sports, especially Pittsburgh sports. What I have learned most of all in team sports is that team members knowing *what* they are to do, *why* they are to do it, *how* they are to do it, and *when* they are to do it is incredibly important for team success. Losing teams are often confused teams. A well-structured team with mediocre talent often beats a supremely talented team with little structure.

It's not only in the sports arena that structure matters. Structure also matters in marriages and parenting. Marriages in which both husband and wife live according to an agreed-upon structure are always stronger than confusing marriages in which the rules and roles always change. Children who grow up in a structured routine virtually always grow up happier and healthier than those who grow up in chaotic households.

When it comes to writing, the best authors are the ones who follow the clearest structure, even if that structure is creative free verse. Good structure in writing leads to the clear communication of ideas, and the clearest books often best help us understand new concepts and possibilities, even if they aren't necessarily the most popular. Music also needs structure. Think of your favorite songs. They often not only have a hook—a melody and phrasing that catches your attention—but they also have a strong structure that makes listening easy.

Structure is crucial to life. All healthy organisms have a clear structure that allows for growth and functioning. Even in our spiritual lives, we need a sense of structure that sets a time, place, and practice for prayer, reflection, and study, and balances our activities, commitments, and demands.

Good worship has a well thought-out structure that takes into consideration both the needs of the worshipers and the talents of the worship leaders. I am not saying that we have to do worship "decently and in order," which is often the motto of Presbyterians. To do things decently and in order can mean adhering to a strict order that stifles ardor. Structure is not the same thing as order, although they are related. Order has to do with arranging elements in a sequential way, while structure generally means creating the parameters that allow for growth. A simple example comes from growing tomatoes. They grow best when staked up rather than being allowed to grow along the ground. An external structure leads to healthy tomatoes. Failure to provide an external structure leads to blighted tomatoes.

Often the structures churches use for worship were created for another time and place. They have been handed down through generations or are adapted from churches that have created their structure in response to their own time and place. In each instance, the structure might not fit our context. This leads to several questions. Reflect on your own worship service. What is the purpose of your worship service's structure? What is it trying to do, and for whom? Does it fit the worshipers and the worship leaders, or some other context? How often do we ask if we have the proper worship structure for our present time, place, and context?

If you will forgive me for offering another sports analogy, I witnessed a great example of the difference the right fit between structure and context can make. As I write this, I am still basking in the glow of witnessing my beloved Pittsburgh Penguins hockey team win the National Hockey League championship, or, as hockey fans know it better, the Stanley Cup. In 2008 the Penguins made it to the championship finals, only to lose to the Detroit Red Wings. The Penguins looked terrible against the Red Wings for much of those finals. The Red Wings seemed quicker, more talented, and just plain better. In 2009, after struggling for much of the season, the Penguins hired a new coach who brought with him a new structure—an offensive structure that suited the Penguins' talent, which was young, quick, and offensively explosive. The previous coach had a strong structure, but it was a defensive one. When they played a defensive style, they couldn't take advantage of their strengths. The new coach brought a new structure. Instead of sitting back and playing defense, the players use their speed to aggressively pressure the other team all over the ice. Their new structure forced the other team to react faster, causing the players to make mistakes that allowed the Penguins to score goals. So, in 2009 the Penguins again played the Red Wings in the finals. This time their structure meshed with their talents, and they managed to beat the Red Wings, defying all the experts who said that the Red Wings were too talented and experienced. The difference was that in 2009 the Penguins, who had a clear structure in the 2008 season, adopted a structure that fit much more effectively with their personnel. There are lessons here for worship.

Worship that leads people to encounter and experience the Holy is structured to meet people where they are spiritually. I believe that an intentionally integrated approach to worship allows worship leaders to create a structure that more effectively reaches those seeking an experience of the Divine. It allows us to make choices based on what opens people both to Christ within and the Spirit all around. I have been inspired and heavily influenced by the writings of the Quaker mystic Thomas Kelly, who said:

> Deep within us all there is an amazing inner sanctuary of the soul, a holy place, a Divine Center, a speaking Voice, to which we may continuously return. Eternity is at our hearts, pressing upon our time-torn lives, warming us with intimations of an as-

tounding destiny, calling us home unto Itself. Yielding to these
persuasions, gladly committing ourselves in body and soul, ut-
terly and completely, to the Light Within, is the beginning of true
life. It is a dynamic center, a creative Life that presses to birth
within us. It is a Light Within which illumines the face of God
and casts new shadows and new glories upon the face of men.
It is a seed stirring to life if we do not choke it. It is the Shekinah
of the soul, the Presence in the midst. Here is the Slumbering
Christ, stirring to be awakened, to become the soul we clothe in
earthly form and action. And He is within us all.[1]

Holy worship attempts to awaken the Slumbering Christ so that
people can experience both the Divine within themselves and the
Divine within fellow worshipers, as well as the Divine emerging
through the hymns they sing together, the prayers they utter, and
the sermons they hear. Structure matters because the right structure can awaken the Slumbering Christ so that the life of Christ
grows in worshipers. Certainly the individual worshiper bears a
responsibility to be personally open, but that has to do with his
or her own structure—his or her own personal commitment to
openness in worship. Despite the responsibility of individuals
to bring a sense of commitment and passion to worship, how a
church structures its worship makes a huge difference in helping
people take that extra step of personal involvement in worship.
There is no right structure for worship, just as in sports, music,
architecture, or families there is no right structure. The best structure is the one that fits the worshipers and worship leaders. With
that said, certain principles of structure are crucial, and we will
focus on them here.

Integrated worship services have a structure that offers a
sense of *balance*. Too often church worship services are unbalanced. Worship services that lack *balance* can cause worshipers to
feel trapped by songs or oratories that never end, to feel caught
in worship spaces that are overwhelming or uninspiring, and
to feel stuck in rituals that are confusing and chaotic. Our focus
here will be on how we can create intentionally integrated worship services that have a balanced structure that enables people
to connect with the Holy in worship.

How Do We Bring Balance to Worship?

What first got me thinking about bringing balance to worship were my experiences trying to help couples create meaningful marriage services. In working with couples to create their weddings, one of my principles is to have traditional elements as well as unique, personal elements. So, while they may process into the sanctuary to traditional music and sing a traditional hymn (although I encourage contemporary songs, too), I often ask them to look for opportunities to create new rituals. For example, I remember working on a wedding service with one couple. The groom was getting a Ph.D in classics, the study of ancient cultures and literature, and he really liked an ancient Roman ritual in which the mothers of the bride and groom would go to the couple's new home during the ceremony and light the hearth so that the house would be warm when the couple got there. The ceremony took place at a new wedding facility that had a fireplace, so we created a ritual in which the mothers brought candles forward and gave them to two ushers, who then lit twenty candles placed in the hearth of the fireplace.

At another wedding, the groom was a biochemist and, as a result, had a fascination with brewing beer. We created a ritual in which I first spoke about how brewing beer served as a metaphor for forming a healthy marriage. On a table to the side of the chancel we had a large empty jug surrounded by four carafes, each with an element needed for brewing beer: malt, hops, yeast, and water. I told the congregation that like the elements of beer, the elements of a good marriage must blend together. For instance, malt is a sugar and gives sweetness to beer. I said that it is like the romance of a marriage. Couples need sweetness for a marriage to work. Hops add a bitter flavor that gives the beer character, and that just like beer, marriages can't have sweetness only. The times of bitterness, struggle, and pain in a marriage all give character to it, especially if the couple is willing to work through them. Most beer brewers will tell you that the water used in beer is key. Poor quality water leads to terrible tasting beer. I said that the water is like the living water of Christ that must be in a relationship. If that water is pure, the flavor of the marriage will always grow better. Finally, I said that the yeast is like the passage of time. If couples are willing to let the sweetness, bitterness, and God's presence mingle, the passage of time will make the marriage ferment into a relationship that is always becoming better. Afterwards, we invited the parents of the bride and groom to come forward and pour the elements into the empty jug. The couple walked forward and sealed the jug with the idea that it would ferment over the course of the next year, and they would drink it together on their first anniversary.

I try to balance personal elements with traditional elements, such as a classical piece for the processional ("Jesu, Joy of Man's Desiring"), a prayer of confession, Scripture reading, the vows, sharing of the rings, and benediction. In the process of trying to help couples create weddings that were both appropriately traditional and personal, I slowly realized that what makes all worship services work is how well balanced they are. The problem in too many worship services is that they offer too much of one element and not enough of another. A worship service will drag if it has too much speaking, too much singing, or too much ritual, causing us to feel as though that portion of worship will never end. I suppose this is a reason that people often complain that sermons are too long. The problem is that the sermons aren't necessarily balanced by other parts of the service that give worshipers a break from an overabundance of speaking. Worshipers can feel like they are listening to someone speak for too long, and as a result they get restless. Longer sermons are more often accepted in congregations when the worshipers feel they are balanced by music. Even within sermons, a balance of teaching, storytelling, showing images and film clips, and bringing in different styles of speaking (using dramatic pauses and inflections, moving out from behind the pulpit, and using a full voice register rather than simply speaking in a monotone), help people pay attention.

I have identified seven areas of balance that I think are crucial to creating an integrated worship service. Balance is a tricky thing because it is an intuitive concept. It is much easier to aim for one pole of the balance continuum or the other, which is why so many churches opt for *either* traditional or contemporary worship. Striking a balance between competing ideas is difficult. Yet holy worship often means finding the right balance that allows people to find an integrative center where disparate elements—from contemporary to traditional, all of which open us to God's presence—can come together to help people experience the Holy.

Area 1: Balance between Music and the Spoken Word

Over the course of my career as a pastor, I have come to believe that balancing music and speaking is the most crucial balancing act in our worship services. How well do churches balance music and the spoken word? Too often they don't do it well. I'm not sure why. Typically, traditional Christian worship, especially traditional Protestant worship, is overly wordy. My guess is that the reason has something to do with the difficulty of finding competent musicians. Finding people who can read well is much easier than finding those who can sing or play an instrument. But I have to be honest. I don't know the reason. The reasons could very well be biblical, although Paul does advise that each of us should "be filled with the Spirit, as you sing psalms and hymns and spiritual songs among yourselves, singing and making melody to the Lord in your hearts, giving thanks to God the Father at all times and for everything in the name of our Lord Jesus Christ" (Eph. 5:18–20). Whatever the reason, the result is that in most denominations, the worship services are very wordy. I believe this is especially true of my tradition, the Presbyterian tradition. We are incredibly wordy, which means that our worship services can feel incredibly slow and plodding.

Start with the typical call to worship for most mainline denominational churches. It is a written, responsive ritual in which a leader reads aloud a printed phrase and the congregation reads aloud a printed response. The congregation might then sing a hymn, but afterwards it reads aloud a prayer of confession, after which a pastor offers a spoken assurance of pardon. Perhaps next an anthem is sung. This anthem is followed by one or more Scripture readings, a children's sermon, an adult sermon, and then a pastoral prayer. This is followed by a benediction. Somewhere in the mix, a hymn and offertory might have been sung. The point is that in most traditional worship services, the time spent speaking way outweighs that spent in music by a factor of two or three to one.

I believe that much of the boredom people experience in traditional worship is that the wordiness of it all wears them out. Modern people are a musical people. Our lives are filled with music that we hear on the radio, computers, iPods, and televisions and in movies, waiting rooms, restaurants, and more. Sermons and prayers and assurances and litanies can also be so abstract and esoteric that people have a hard time with all those words. We simply aren't built for listening to that many words without something else to balance them. Think about almost all the mediums we participate in that feature people speaking, especially in dialogue with each other. The speaking is often balanced with other elements. For instance, in television shows and films, music underscores the words, letting us know whether they are important, silly, scary, or potentially harmful to the characters or the situation. Vivid visual images also are prominent in television. For instance, in documentaries, we see alternating images as narrators, subjects, and experts talk, while both words and images are underscored by music. Articles on the Internet seem to be kept intentionally short. Unlike two centuries ago, people today seem to be neurologically wired to absorb oral (or printed, in this case) information only for a short time. Modern media, especially television, has shaped our brains to absorb a broad-band of information (visual, auditory, tactile) at the same time, but this has diminished our ability to focus on one source of information (especially oral or printed) for long periods of time. Recognizing the fact that people have short attention spans for one source of information, I often use PowerPoint presentations to show pictures or maps, or to present bullet points when I preach. The visuals capture people's attention. Wordiness loses people's attention.

Knowing all this, I am particularly sensitive to how wordy much of traditional worship is and how insensitive many mainline pastors are to this wordiness. For instance, I have been to many conferences and workshops where the worship bulletins are filled with words, and every ritual is a responsive litany or reading. Often church committee meetings begin with a devotional, and most people choose to read something to us, which causes us to space out. I'm personally just not that good at listening to someone read for a long time.

Meanwhile, contemporary worship seems like an overreaction to this traditional worship dominance of word over music. Thus, most contemporary worship services overcompensate in the opposite way as music eclipses words two to one. The complaint I hear most often from people who don't like contemporary worship is that they feel forced to stand and sing for twenty minutes at the start of a worship service, and that there is just too much music—much of it sounding exactly the same.

I understand what those putting together contemporary worship are trying to do. They intuitively understand that traditional worship has been too wordy and that today's culture is musically oriented. So, they try to create a musical experience very, very different from the wordiness of traditional worship. Few contemporary worship services have prolonged periods of speaking. The only prolonged period is the sermon, and it is expected to be short and to the point.

Integrated worship strikes a balance between word and music. It recognizes that people cannot attend to one mode for too long. Sometimes the music is a short refrain sung by the congregation in response to something else. Sometimes it is a hymn. Sometimes it is an anthem or other piece of music that worshipers listen to. The point is balancing spoken words with some sort of music, and balancing music with spoken words. The key is striking the right *balance,* and balance is elusive and subjective. When seeking balance, a perfect balancing point rarely exists. For those who love words, anything but the bare minimum in music seems unbalanced. For those who love music, anything but the minimum time necessary for speaking is unbalanced. The point here is not to aim for some mythical perfection in balance, but to find ways to be intentional about striking a balance between how much is spoken in words and how much is experienced through music.

Pages 116-117 give an example, with commentary, of a typical Calvin Presbyterian Church worship service that shows how we try to keep this balance.

| Gathering Hymn[A] | "Step by Step" | Songbook #113 |

Welcome and Prayer Concerns

Opening Chant[B]
The Lord is my song, the Lord is my prayer. All my hope comes from God.
The Lord is my song, the Lord is my prayer, God, the wellspring of life.

Time of Quiet Prayer and Prayer of Blessing[C]

| Hymn of Praise[D] | "Here I Am, Lord" | Hymnal #525 |

Prayer of Humility[E]
Gracious and eternal God, you hope that we would live whole, holy, and healthy lives. Why, then, do we excel at living fragmented, sinful, and unhealthy lives? Why do we struggle so much to be loving, caring, gentle, patient, and kind? There are so many opportunities in life where we could respond better to you and others. Instead, we let our lives slip, if just a little, by giving in to hurry, irritation, and anxiety. Instead of responding with loving-kindness, we give people sharp retorts. Instead of being gently patient, we impatiently criticize. Give us your heart so that we can give others your love. Hear us as we offer you our silent prayer.
(Continue by offering your silent confession.)

Confession Response[F]
O Lord, hear my prayer; O Lord, hear my prayer. When I call, answer me.
O Lord, hear my prayer; O Lord, hear my prayer. Come and listen to me.

Assurance of God's Love
L. Friends, believe the Good News of the Gospel.
P: In Jesus Christ we are forgiven!

Congregational Response   Doxology
Praise God, from whom all blessings flow; Praise Him, all creatures here below;
Praise Him above, ye heavenly host; Praise Father, Son, and Holy Ghost. Amen

| Scripture | Ephesians 4:25–5:2 | p. 194 NT |

L: This is the Word of the Lord.
P: Thanks be to God.

Children's Sermon

Anthem[G]

Sermon   **"The Peril of Anger"**

Offering/Offertory

| Prayer of Dedication[H] | "Give Thanks" | Written by Henry Smith |

Pastoral Prayer and Lord's Prayer
L: The Lord be with you.
P: And also with you.[I]

| Closing Hymn[J] | "If You Are the Vine" | Songbook #121 |

Blessing and Benediction[K]

Response   *"Amen, Amen"*

Postlude

A. This is always a contemporary, "up" song, designed to offer praise and to bring people together with a good sense of energy before beginning worship. It imitates the beginning of most contemporary worship services.

B. An opening chant, sung three times, using either a Taizé chant or a refrain from a hymn or contemporary song.

C. A time of silent prayer followed by a spoken prayer from the front by a worship leader. The prayer blesses the congregation and asks God to be present in our worship.

D. This is always a more traditional song taken from *The Presbyterian Hymnal*. *Traditional* can mean many things. For many in our church, "Here I Am, Lord," a song written in 1981 by Daniel Schutte, is traditional since it comes from a hymnal rather than a contemporary songbook.

E. Said in unison. This is a prayer of confession, basically, but we call it the "Prayer of Humility" to allow us to write the prayer more broadly. Our understanding is that confession is an act of humility, but humility is more than just confession.

F. This is a Taizé chant or song refrain that is sung once. Sometimes, if a chant or song has two verses, we will use the chant as both an opening chant and confession response.

G. Sung by a choir, a soloist, or a duet, or played as an instrumental.

H. Here we print the words to the refrain of "Give Thanks" by Henry Smith, (Integrity's Hosannah Music, 1978).

I. After this response, either the choir sings a small piece called "Holy, Holy, Holy," or it is played meditatively on a piano.

J. A hymn or song chosen to fit most closely with the passage for the day.

K. The congregation stands, holds hands, and the pastor says a prayer of blessing over the congregation, followed by a traditional benediction.

Appreciating the balance I'm talking about just by looking at an order for worship is hard, yet you can at least glimpse it. Something that you may notice is that if you count the number of songs in this service, you will see we sing almost as many as in a typical contemporary service, but because word and song are more in balance, the number is not as noticeable. If you include the prelude and postlude, this service has at least twelve pieces of music. Some are long, some are very short, yet there is a great variety. You will also notice that short spoken parts of worship are often balanced by short sung pieces. Longer spoken pieces are often followed by longer sung pieces.

Area 2: Balance between Performance and Participation

Performance and participation is another area often out of balance in worship. Performance is any part of the service that requires little from the congregation other than to be attentive and appreciative, such as a sermon, anthem, or spoken prayer. A great or meaningful performance does connect people with the Holy, so there is nothing wrong with performance. But too much performance in worship can cause people to feel like they are watching a play rather than participating in worship. Performance needs to be balanced by participation. Performance can open people to the Holy by presenting something inspiring that connects the mind, heart, and soul with the Divine, but it does so vicariously. When we watch a great performance of a singer or a preacher, we connect with God through that person.

In contrast with performance, participation connects us with God through an act that engages us physically. We participate in a worship service when we sing a hymn, a song, or a chant; say a written or memorized prayer together; respond aloud to a part of the worship service (such as receiving the worship leader's salutation, "The Lord be with you," by offering our own greeting, *"And also with you"*); or engaging in a ritual or sacrament. Too much participation can feel rote or even manipulative, but too little participation can cause a worship service to feel barren.

Looking at the order of worship on pages 116-117 you will notice a few stretches when participation and performance are not balanced in some way. The balance isn't always one to one; that is, a performance is not always followed by a participatory act. Instead, the balance may be achieved in larger segments. For instance, the early part of the service—from the gathering song, the greeting and sharing of prayer concerns that takes place during the "Welcome and Prayer Concerns," the singing of the opening hymn, the chant, the personal time of quiet prayer, the spoken "Prayer of Humility," the personal and silent prayer of confession, the sung confession response, and the sung "Doxology"—is mostly participatory. Afterwards, a long stretch—from the Scripture reading, through the children's sermon (although this may be participatory for the children), anthem, and sermon—is more performance-like. After the sermon, the ratio of performance and participation is nearly one to one, with an offering, a sung response, a prayer of dedication, a pastoral prayer, a communal Lord's Prayer, a hymn, a blessing and benediction, and another sung response.

The whole point is to be intentional about balancing performance and participation. Sometimes both contemporary and traditional worship can feel like performances, even when the music is participatory. Part of the balance has to do with the kinds of participation. In the order on pages 116-117, worshipers participate by singing together, speaking together, and speaking privately. I do not pretend that what I have presented is the best or only way to reach this balance. Instead, it is one example of the balance between performance and participation.

AREA 3: BALANCE BETWEEN STIMULATION AND CENTERING

Another common imbalance in both contemporary and traditional worship is between elements meant to stimulate and those meant to center worshipers. Simply put, the focus of contemporary worship is generally to stimulate worshipers. I think much of contemporary worship is like Top 40 music, which attempts to score spiritual "hits" or "hooks" that grab people and get them excited. Even the term for most contemporary music—*praise* music—suggests that it is meant to stimulate. The problem is that the focus on energizing people can cause them to confuse stimulation with inspiration. Just because a piece of music stimulates worshipers does not mean that it inspires them. But people often confuse the two, because in our spiritually immature era, inspirations are assumed to be adrenaline-surging experiences. This has not always been the case. Many mystics found their inspirations to be centering, calming, stilling experiences. Thomas Kelly captures perfectly how inspirations come in centering rather than through stimulation:

> There is a way of ordering our mental life on more than one level at once. On one level we may be thinking, discussing, seeing, calculating, meeting all the demands of external affairs. But deep within, behind the scenes, at a profounder level, we may also be in prayer and adoration, song and worship and a gentle receptiveness to divine breathings.
>
> The secular world of today values and cultivates only the first level, assured that *there* is where the real business of mankind is done, and scorns, or smiles in tolerant amusement, at the cultivation of the second level—a luxury enterprise, a vestige of superstition, an occupation for special temperaments. But in a deeply religious culture men know that the deep level of prayer and of divine attendance is the most important thing in the world. It is at this deep level that the real business of life is determined. The secular mind is an abbreviated, fragmentary mind, building only upon a part of man's nature and neglecting a part—the most glorious part—of man's nature, powers, and resources. The religious mind involves the whole of man, embraces his relations with time within their true ground and setting in the Eternal Lover. It ever keeps close to the fountains of divine creativity.[2]

I certainly don't want to suggest that people cannot experience inspirations in ways that also stimulate. I just believe that a balance is needed. In many ways, traditional worship seems to emphasize some form of centering stillness. In the most traditional worship services, worshipers are expected to enter in silence, and the aim of the service seems to be to quiet and calm the person so that she can sense God. I am convinced that so many of the traditional hymns of the past were written in a manner and meter meant to slow life down. The problem with a service so focused on centering is that for those of us used to constant stimulation, like most people in our culture, the service doesn't feel as though it is centering. It feels stifling. Just as people in contemporary worship can confuse stimulation with inspiration, people in traditional worship can confuse seriousness with centeredness, missing out on one of the good things about stimulating praise music: it emphasizes a joy and lightness that traditional worship often loses. Contemporary worship teaches people that faith and worship can be an uplifting experience.

The point is that contemporary worship often focuses on stimulation and joy, while traditional worship often focuses on centering and seriousness. My vision is that integrated worship incorporates a fluidity between praise and centering. Some elements, such as a praise song, a solo, a story from a sermon, or a movie clip, stir and excite us; other elements, such as times of silence, confession, communion, or prayer, center us. A fluidity in worship between stimulation and centering allows us to move in both directions. At times we will be stimulated to smile, laugh, and experience joy. At other times we will be stilled, awed, and calmed in order to experience God and "know . . . the deep level of prayer and of divine attendance" that Thomas Kelly speaks about.

AREA 4: BALANCE BETWEEN TYPES OF MUSIC

The 1992 film *Sister Act*, starring Whoopi Goldberg, tells the story of a lounge singer who witnesses a mob crime and is hidden by police as a nun in a convent. The local parish to which the convent is attached is struggling, so the woman decides to help the choir. She gets a very traditional choir to sing contemporary pop songs that she has transformed into praise songs. For instance, she teaches the choir to sing the Supremes' song "My Guy," substituting "My God" for "My Guy." The film was a major hit and conversation piece among many Christians because it brought contemporary pop into a worship service. Many people loved the film precisely because it advocated a greater variety of music.

Our worship music often has little variation. For example, contemporary Christian music has a fairly homogenous sound. The reason is that much of it emerged out of the Nashville music scene through artists such as Steven Curtis Chapman, Amy Grant, Michael W. Smith, and Third Day. Their roots were clearly country, and their audience was largely white, Southern evangelical and Pentecostal churches. Thus, they influenced the sound of much contemporary praise music. In the same way, much of traditional Christian hymnody is influenced by European-style classical music, and much of African American gospel music was shaped by sounds coming out of the South at the end of the nineteenth and beginning of the twentieth centuries. The result has been that most worship services tend to offer a homogenous selection of hymns, songs, and anthems.

The contradiction is that we live in an incredibly diverse musical culture today. People listen to a wide variety of musical genres, from pop to rock, country, jazz, grunge, metal, alternative, blues, rhythm and blues, hip hop, folk, classical, and beyond. Music in worship should take advantage of all the different musical forms people listen to. This is a very difficult balance to strike because it requires music leaders with a variety of talents. Many church musicians are experienced in only one form or a few. For example, many mainline churches employ music directors with a background more in classical music than in contemporary. And many contemporary worship music directors have backgrounds in one style of music, which may be a country-rooted kind of Christian contemporary song. Finding music directors who are adept at a whole variety of styles is difficult, which means that the answer may be to spend more on hiring several directors who can direct various choirs, groups, and soloists.

In the worship service at Calvin Presbyterian, we try to offer a variety of music. Some forms predominate because they are the forms that our music leaders are most comfortable with, but we stretch ourselves. We will play and sing classical and traditional hymns, contemporary songs, Broadway tunes, blues songs (sometimes changing the words), jazz pieces, meditative pieces, white and black gospel, and other forms of music, including traditional hymns played in a contemporary meter. And we typically do so in a way that *counterpoints* other pieces in the service. For instance, if our choir sings a very up-tempo gospel song as an anthem, we may sing a meditative version of a classical hymn as the offertory. As mentioned before, our gathering hymn is always contemporary, and our opening hymn is always traditional. We try to be intentional in our integration of music so that we do not employ the same kinds of songs throughout worship, but make sure each song is a counterpoint to other songs in a service. This gives the service a kind of fluidity and balance.

The counterpointing can go along several continuums, such as traditional to contemporary, up-tempo to down-tempo, classical to blues or gospel or rhythm and blues, and energetic to meditative. The point is to use balance to create a kind of flow, a rhythm that moves throughout the service, from stimulation to centering and all experiences in-between. There is no right way to strike this balance, only intentionality in seeking this balance, which is something that wise worship leaders seek.

Area 5. Balance between Tradition, Retradition, and New Tradition

When should a church honor a tradition, and when should we create a new one? A tradition is a practice or perspective that transmits a set of beliefs and perceptions across generations. Once a particular ritual or practice becomes established, it becomes a tradition, but every tradition was new at one point. In modern culture—not just religion—people adhere to age-old traditions all the time. They also retradition them by creating new ways of practicing and expressing these traditions. In addition, they constantly create new traditions that express new ideas. But how do we in the church decide when a worship tradition should be retraditioned or when a practice or perspective should be adopted as a new tradition?

For a healthy, holy worship service, churches need to keep a balance between observing old traditions, retraditioning them, and adopting new practices that might become traditions. At times, we need to adhere to age-old traditions that people are used to, because they still retain their power to connect people with the Holy. For instance, most mainline Protestant worship services include a smattering of traditions that have endured throughout Christian history. The responsive litany at the beginning of the Sacrament of Holy Communion is a great example:

> L: The Lord be with you.
> P: *And also with you.*
> L: Lift up your hearts.
> P: *We lift them up to the Lord our God.*
> L: Let us give thanks to the Lord our God.
> P: *It is right to give thanks and praise.*

Denominations use minor variations on this, but it is a consistent tradition rooted in a common Hebrew greeting and dating back to early Christian liturgies. As ancient as this exchange is, it has at times been recreated in ways that were consistent with a new age. A simple example of that retraditioning would be from the Protestant movement, when pastors began to preach in the common language of worshipers instead of Latin, as had been the custom prior to the Reformation. No longer did the pastor say, "*Dominus vobiscum*," and worshipers respond, "*Et cum spiritu tuo.*"

While retraditioning is often desirable, there are periods when new traditions are needed. The whole contemporary worship movement has become an established tradition, and some form of contemporary worship will probably be with us for centuries. Contemporary worship is a new creation that emphasizes alternative music forms and structures worship much like a concert. Taizé worship also is a new tradition that is quickly becoming an established one. Our struggle is knowing when to maintain a tradition, when to engage in a retraditioning, and when to create a new tradition.

We created a new tradition at Calvin Presbyterian Church several years ago that was an amalgamation of several other traditions, and we did it in response to the concerns of both members and our worship leaders. As our church grew and attracted younger members, the sanctuary became noisier prior to worship. The fact is that members of the baby boom generation and younger don't have the traditional reverence for worship spaces that previous generations did. Older generations entered worship in silence and sat or kneeled in prayer. The period prior to worship was meant to be a time of quiet centering. Some older members came to me with complaints that the sanctuary had become very noisy prior to worship. I often responded that I didn't know what to do, because I couldn't see myself standing up before worship and saying to people, "Okay, folks, quiet down. This is a time for quiet prayer, so shut up!" That is not the way to make people of the younger generations feel welcome.

At the same time, the way our church, most other Presbyterian churches, and many other denominational churches started their worship bugged me. I have always hated traditional calls to worship, which are usually written litanies between a worship leader and the congregation. They violate many of my personal rules for worship because they are wordy and stilted, and reading the words rarely expressed the enthusiasm for worship I believe the words intend to convey. The worship leader can say, with great enthusiasm, "We worship the Lord today!" and the congregation responds in an unemotional and disengaged voice: "Yes, today we worship with great joy." They never sound as though they feel joy. In fact, they often sound like robots.

Combining my frustration with these calls to worship and the complaints of older members seeking more quiet and reverence, I began to ask if there was a way to address both problems. Our worship committee discussed this at length, and we came up with a new way to begin worship. After our announcements, we would sing a Taizé or Taizé-like chant, which would quiet and center people. Following that, we would enter about thirty seconds of quiet prayer, giving people an opportunity to pray in silence and to prepare themselves for worship. Then one of our worship leaders would come forward and say a prayer of blessing over the congregation that would go much like this:

> Holy God, as we gather in your presence, bless us with your grace so that in worship today we can sense, hear, and experience you. Open our minds, hearts, and souls so that this worship will lead us to follow you in everything. In Christ's name we pray. Amen.

We created a new tradition for our church that addressed what we saw as problems in our worship.

In the process, we also reconnected the church with an ancient tradition that had been lost until the advent of Taizé worship—a style of worship that formed in France as a result of the work of Roger Louis Schütz-Marsauche, who later became known as Brother Roger. He wanted to create a sort of ecumenical monastic community that bridged the abyss between Roman Catholic and Protestant practices. Knowing that Roman Catholics and Protestants could not share communion together, and that in the Roman Catholic tradition only priests could read the Gospels and preach in worship, he had to come up with an order of worship that didn't violate any denomination's rules. So he recovered the ancient tradition of chanting, which was how the early Christians sang. Since most early Christians didn't read, they would memorize phrases of psalms, lines of Scripture, or written verses, and chant them over and over. Taizé worship does just this. Worshipers typically gather and sing a variety of chants, then spend time in spoken and quiet prayer, sing more chants, then read Scripture and take time for quiet reflection, and then sing more chants. This was a new tradition that recovered an ancient tradition. We adapted these chants to our purposes, using them as a way to begin our worship, which simultaneously connects us to both the ancient tradition of chanting and the new tradition of Taizé worship.

Practicing certain worship traditions binds people together. But the question is whether churches adhere rigidly to old traditions, retradition them to meet new generations, or create new traditions to bind people in new practices. Integrated worship brings together ancient, classic, contemporary, and experimental traditions. The key question is always, what will lead people to experience and encounter the Holy?

AREA 6: BALANCE BETWEEN COMPLEXITY AND SIMPLICITY

I don't know how often it has happened, but I have experienced far too many worship rituals that failed because of their complexity. Typically, these rituals don't fail in Sunday worship, because most pastors don't experiment on Sundays. I typically experience these difficult worship services when I go to a conference, seminar, or retreat—places where everyone experiments.

For example, during a worship service at one conference, each worshiper was given a piece of paper upon which we were to write down our hopes and dreams. Then we were to write down our greatest misgivings about our hopes and dreams. Then we were to name all the dreams that we had failed to accomplish. Then we were to come to the front of the worship space and form a circle, where we lifted those dreams toward God, asking God to lift up our dreams. Then we were asked to put the slips of paper in our pockets and hold onto them as a reminder that God promises to be with us in our dreams.

What was the problem? With so many instructions, and the thoughts to write down on the paper so expansive, it just seemed too big for what we were doing. By the time we were called to the front, I was frustrated and only wrote on my paper, "My dream is to not do this! My misgivings are that I am doing this! The dream I have failed to accomplish is being somewhere else!" When we stood in the circle, I halfheartedly held my dream sheet aloft, wishing I had skipped the worship service. The service was way too complex, with far too many instructions, and asked me to manufacture a sincerity I wasn't ready to offer.

Integrative worship balances complexity and simplicity. It always seeks to address complex thoughts, emotions, and practices in the simplest ways. In other words, worship leaders teach complex theological concepts, touch people's varied emotions, and lead them through orchestrated rituals, but we try to do so in ways that are relatively easy to grasp and embrace. The truth is that all humans seek simplicity. For instance, think about the most powerful political sentiments. They are often articulated bumper-sticker style. That doesn't necessarily make the ideas right, but it does make them powerful. People seek simplicity in life, even if they keep adding complexities that, ironically, make their lives more hassled. I am convinced that people believe being rich will make their lives better because they think the wealthy—who can afford maids to clean, cooks to cook, and butlers to serve—live simpler lives. What they don't realize is that most wealthy people struggle, because they feel their lives are too complex.

Overly complex worship overwhelms. One of the reasons contemporary worship is so popular among younger generations is that it offers simplicity. The songs have simple melodies and can be easily grasped and sung. The structure of worship is simple—songs, prayer, and preaching. Even the preaching, which is intended to be seeker-friendly, distills complex Christian beliefs into simple, easy-to-understand phrases or formulas. It offers an effective model of communication that the mainline church too often ignores.

I believe that the mainline church often suffers from complexity. Our worship services combine various elements and rituals that can be confusing, especially for someone who is new to Christian worship. Even our preaching can be complex. Many seminary-trained pastors preach complex sermons emphasizing theological ideas and concepts that they just assume members understand. In fact, one of the biggest problems in mainline preaching is that pastors love to explore theological issues and problems, but have a hard time offering practical, livable answers to them. We pastors love the questions, but aren't comfortable providing answers.

Other elements of traditional mainline worship are often complex. I think classically based music is complex for modern culture. Reading too many passages of Scripture in one service can be complex, especially if the different passages don't mesh—if the Old Testament reading, psalm, epistle, and Gospel all seem to be about different topics. Reading different passages that seem to have no connection with each other loses the worshiper. Take time to reflect on your own worship services. How complex are they in terms of rituals, readings, preaching, and music?

I am not advocating that churches reduce worship to the simplest terms. What I am advocating is that we look for ways to balance complexity and simplicity. We need to always ask, is what we are doing too complex for people, or is it okay to expect people to work to understand something complex? The idea is not to become simplistic. There are times when complexity is good. I find that Christmas Eve services and some special services are much more complex, but they come at a time when people are looking for a richer experience. Still, the key is balance.

Let me give you an example of what I mean by balance. During the first worship service at Calvin Presbyterian, we offer communion every Sunday. Once a month we offer healing prayers as part of the communion service. Typically, we Presbyterians distribute the elements to worshipers as they remain seated in the pews. The way we practice communion can present a problem if we are to offer healing prayers, since typically people come forward to be prayed over by a pastor or one trained in prayer. The problem arises when we distribute the elements to people in the pews, while also asking people to leave their pews and come forward to pray. I have spoken to several pastors who have offered healing prayers in this way, and I have attended services done in this manner. The problem is that this method of combining prayer and communion is too complex. We would be asking people to break away from one action (receiving communion while sitting) to take part in a separate action (coming forward for prayer). We would also be asking people to go against the flow of traffic in the sanctuary by coming forward. In addition, coming forward could result in their becoming the focus of speculation—"Why is so-and-so going up for prayer?"

Our answer? We ask everyone to come forward for communion down our two aisles, much like people do in Roman Catholic, Episcopal, and Lutheran traditions, and we invite those who want healing prayers to step out of line and move to a central area in front of our chancel to receive prayers from one of our prayer ministers. After receiving prayer, they simply step back into line and receive communion, which allows taking communion to also be part of the healing ritual. Because people are focused on either standing in line to receive communion, praying while waiting to come forward, or returning to their seats to pray, their focus is more on the sacrament, not the person receiving prayers. Also, a simple flow of people going forward and returning simplifies the ritual for everyone. This is what I mean by a balance between complexity and simplicity. We are complicating communion by adding healing prayers, but we are trying to do so in a way that feels natural.

One of the best rituals I was ever part of is one I brought back to our church to use in worship. I was at a conference, and the preacher spoke about baptism and how through our baptisms we were created anew, even if we weren't aware of who we were. She told us that each baptism is a cleansing that lasts throughout eternity, and that in remembering we are baptized, we are brought into union with Christ. Afterwards, we were invited into a ritual in which we renewed our baptismal vows as a recommitment to serve God in our lives. We then were invited to walk down the aisle to the front of the chancel where a crystal glass bowl filled with small, clear, drop-shaped pebbles in water had been placed on a stand. We were to reach into the water and pull out a pebble, keeping it to remind us that we are a new creation. Afterwards, we sang together the hymn "Baptized in Water." I found this ritual to be very moving because of the simple way it communicated the complexity of baptism. Eight years later, I still have that pebble sitting on the dresser in my bedroom. The key is that the simplicity of the ritual opened us all to a deep, spiritual, mysterious complexity.

Area 7: Balance between Gravity and Levity

A final balancing act in worship is between gravity and levity. I find that far too many traditional worship services have an oppressive sense of gravity. It seems like no one is having any fun. For any endeavor to be worthwhile, I think it must have an element of levity, even if it is something serious. Of course, that sense of levity has to be tempered by the mood of the occasion.

I learned this lesson playing sports. I have played sports on teams with oppressive, serious, critical coaches. Other times I have played on teams with positive, praising, and joy-filled coaches. I always played better on the latter teams because they were fun. I wasn't worried all the time about being perfect. Instead, I was focused on contributing.

I think a similar dynamic goes on in worship. Worship that is all serious and without a sense of cheer is oppressive. For example, a pastor can give a eulogy for a person and talk about how sad the person's death is while still telling funny stories about the person. We can talk about a serious subject and still lighten it a bit with a joke or a funny observation. The lightening can serve to make it easier to digest the seriousness of the topic.

One of the things that the worship staff at Calvin Presbyterian Church emphasizes is that we should have fun with what we are doing, because worship is meant to be joyful. We try to communicate serious messages, but we never forget to laugh in the process. We try hard to make our children's sermons enjoyable, especially through our interactions with the children. We don't experience it as a problem when the children respond to us by saying something annoying or bizarre. We see their spontaneity as creating opportunities to improvise and make the sermons enjoyable. When I preach, I find ways to bring levity into even the most serious of subjects. Perhaps it is through telling a story or a joke or making a silly observation. For instance, if I am preaching about the nastiness of being crucified, and it is obvious that what I am saying is very much a downer, I might add, "As you can see, being crucified definitely ruins your day." I'm not trying to belittle it. I'm trying to bring some levity to a grave subject.

I believe that worship should have a balance between depth and superficiality, seriousness and cheerfulness, sorrow and joy, dark and light, and gravity and levity.

Final Thoughts

Balance is a tricky thing because everyone experiences worship differently. One person's balance is another person's imbalance. For instance, what may bring levity to a worship service for one person may seem irreverent to another. What may seem simple to one person may seem simplistic to another. What may be a new tradition for one may be sacrilegious to another. What may seem like a balance between stimulation and centering for one person may feel either boring or frantic to others. This is what makes worship so hard to do in a multigenerational way. Everyone has his or her own sense of what balance is. Many in the older generations would say that balance for them is *mostly* classical music, maintaining tradition, and taking worship seriously, while younger generations might say that balance for them is *mostly* contemporary songs, trying something new, and being able to laugh.

Thus, integrated worship requires that churches pay attention to the experiences of those worshiping with us, as well as those we hope to attract to worship. Striking a balance often means paying attention to where people are and responding in ways that integrate their worship preferences.

Reflection Questions

1. As you reflect on the whole chapter, what concepts or points stood out for you and why?
2. Looking at the structure of your worship service, discuss how it is or isn't structured to lead people to an encounter with the Holy.
3. To what extent is your church's worship service balanced in terms of
   - music and speaking?
   - performance and participation?
   - stimulation and centering?
   - types of music?
   - tradition, retradition, and new tradition?
   - complexity and simplicity?
   - gravity and levity?
4. Discuss ways of bringing better balance to your worship services.

CHAPTER 6

Leading a Church
toward Holy Worship

DO YOU KNOW WHAT THE BIGGEST PROBLEM IS WITH TRANSFORMING
worship? The biggest problem is that it's not so much *what* we do
as *how* we go about doing it. Too many church leaders believe that
their congregations are resistant to change and transformation,
when what congregations really resist is the way leaders bring
about change and transformation. As I often say, it's not change
that they resist. It's the *pace* of change and the *haste* of change.

Recently, I spoke with a pastor about the conflict she experienced after instituting a number of changes in her congregation,
including some that resulted from suggestions I had made in my
previous books. She was frustrated with the congregation, and
especially with the leadership, because they had really resisted
her ideas. I then asked her to tell me what the leaders did to resist
her suggestions. I listened for about ten minutes and then asked
her how long she had been a pastor at the church. She said that
she had been there only a year. I was shocked. She tried to make
changes in one year that took me seven years. I told her that they
weren't resisting her new ideas so much as they were resisting
the pace of instituting those ideas. She was introducing change
so quickly, so forcefully, and so persistently that they no longer
trusted her, nor felt that she loved and trusted them. It wasn't
a question of what she was doing. It was a question of how she
was doing it.

Much conflict today in the mainline church occurs precisely
because church leaders, and especially pastors, get so focused on
the *what* of change that they forget the *how* of change. The mainline church is rife with conflict regarding worship. A lot of that

conflict has been unnecessary. Most struggling churches recognize that they need to change in order to grow and need to grow in order to remain alive, but the process also feels threatening to members of a congregation who love the way their church is or has been. Most resistance isn't to change but to the way change is instituted.

When change is forced upon a congregation that lacks confidence and faces an uncertain future, especially change from traditional to contemporary worship, one of three outcomes tends to result. The first outcome is that the change is a success at the expense of the members. In some cases, the transition to a new style of worship results in a vibrant worship service that attracts new members, but often older, more traditional members leave the church. I have seen this time and again, as a forceful new pastor comes to a church, bluntly tells the congregation that it will continue declining unless it goes all contemporary, and then succeeds in changing the worship. The problem is that many of the more traditional members feel as though they have been run over. They often leave the church or are even pushed out by a pastor who responds to their concerns by saying that this worship is God's will and that they have to be more seeker-oriented. This statement probably has some truth, but in the process, the leadership has really just chosen one generation over another. Thus, the church has failed to be multigenerational.

A second outcome often occurs when a church decides to add a second, more contemporary worship service. I find this option to be better than the one described above, but it also has its own issues. If the contemporary service is successful, it can cause a church to have, in effect, two separate congregations—one younger, one older—under one roof. Tensions then mount in the leadership as the growing, contemporary congregation with less financial clout (younger generations in general give less than older ones) vies for control with the declining, traditional congregation that has more financial power. The fact is that contemporary worship is more expensive, on average, than traditional worship. It requires better sound and technology, more musicians, and greater expertise than traditional worship. This means that the declining congregation has to fund a growing congregation that seems to disdain the declining one.

A third outcome is a simple one: failure. The attempt either to transform an existing worship service or to start a contemporary one doesn't work. Perhaps the failure is due to lack of talent; for contemporary worship to work, it must be done well. I think it is harder to do well than traditional worship, because contemporary worship requires enhanced coordination between musicians and many more rehearsals. Perhaps the demographics of the area just aren't conducive to contemporary worship. Perhaps the reasons are many. Regardless of the reasons, the failure of the service to catch on can escalate division, as those who were against the service play "I told you so" with those who supported it. Instead of bringing life to the church, the effort moves the church into a dysfunctional phase that diminishes everything.

Regardless of the outcome, the transition to contemporary worship, whether within an existing service or by beginning an alternative one, has an impact on a congregation. Whenever a church decides to offer *either* traditional or contemporary worship, it loses its ability to be multigenerational in its worship because it starts catering to one generation, adding to the existing generational fragmentation that is rampant in our culture. Typically, the congregation divides along generational lines. Some people may not consider that to be a problem, but the division adds to an already increasingly fragmented legacy of worship in North America.

Churches are increasingly becoming divided in worship not only racially and ethnically but also generationally. In fewer and fewer churches do we really find multigenerational worship, at least not of the kind advocated in this book. I certainly don't want to insinuate that contemporary worship is inherently divisive. But church leaders have to be aware that our culture is at odds with itself, and the form of worship churches adopt can either heal the wounds of division in some small way or accentuate the clashes. Thus, leadership is key. Whatever form of worship churches adopt, leaders have to be sensitive to the pain the transition to that worship causes. Good leadership will unite a congregation as it makes that transition, but many leaders end up dividing people in their zeal to achieve their visions.

In the end, transformation leading to worship that works and gives life to a church isn't so much a matter of *what kind* of worship a church does as it is *how* a church is led through the process of transformation. Before exploring how to lead people forward to adopt alternative elements or forms of worship, let's look at why the conflict arises in the first place.

Why Is There So Much Conflict?

The reality of the modern mainline church is that congregations experience a tremendous amount of conflict today. Congregations are not alone in our conflict, though. Our denominations, communities, schools, and culture also deal with a tremendous amount of conflict. Why?

Personally, I believe a major factor is a generational one. Simply put, the baby boom generation, which has always been idealistic and ideological, tends toward conflict. As generational researchers William Strauss and Neil Howe have said, "As Boomers have charted their life's voyage, they have metamorphosed from Beaver Cleaver to hippie to braneater to yuppie to what some are calling 'Neo-Puritan' in a manner quite unlike what anyone, themselves included, ever expected."[1] The authors say this generation is a narcissistic, idealistic cohort that sets it values based on internal, immutable standards of right and wrong.[2] The result is that the generation has always been in conflict with others, whether the conflict was generated by the credo "Trust no one over thirty" or focused on the Vietnam War, the political conflicts of the Republican Revolution, the wars in Iraq and Afghanistan, or the younger generations it considered "slackers" and "lazy."

Right now, baby boomers—those generally born between 1943 and 1963—tend to be the older pastors and leaders of our churches. These leaders have an internal sense of what is right and wrong for a church and are willing to do battle for their causes. When engaging in righteous battle, these combatants rarely consider the validity of their anointed enemies' views. This creates the conditions ripe for conflict in our churches. So, when a new pastor comes into the church, armed with new ideas that the baby boomer members don't understand, it is not surprising that they respond by pushing back. What can create even more conflict is when the pastors themselves have a boomeresque certainty that their vision is the *right* vision.

With all that said, I can't just say that the conflict is due to generational issues. The generational issue suggests what the conflict may be about, but it doesn't get to the root of the conflict. What causes people to push back so harshly when church leaders try to bring about change? The basic answer is *biology.* When we bring about change that people aren't ready for, it often causes people to have a visceral, biological reaction. People don't just choose to become angry. Anger wells up from within them as a defensive reaction against something threatening, and it consumes them.

Psychologist Gregory Lester, one of the preeminent lecturers on personality disorders, has also done a tremendous amount of research on people's emotional reactions to change. He says, "We want others to be rational, decent, and sensible. We want them to see the obvious, to know their impact on and to understand us. We expect them to see the world as we see it. But people often don't. They surprise us. They do things that don't make sense to us. They do things that are so opposed to the way we think things should be done we end up wondering how anyone could do them."[3]

Why do people do those things? Lester says it has to do with basic biology and survival instinct. He says that we are wired to respond biologically to any threat, especially conceptual threats that threaten our beliefs and values, by engaging in actions that will protect us.[4] What distinguishes us from every other animal is that our survival instinct is activated not only by biological threats but also by conceptual threats. We are the only creatures who have self-awareness and self-concepts. We are the only creatures who will defend ourselves against threats to our identities and our ideologies. We are neurologically wired to fight when our concepts are threatened. When a person does or says something that threatens either our self-concept, or a cherished concept, we experience it as a threat to our survival. Animals only have to survive in the biological world. We have to survive in both a biological and a conceptual world, and we can experience death in either realm.[5] It's this sense of survival instinct about concepts that causes people to feel so strongly about religious or political ideals. These ideals help shape our identity, and death to one of these ideals can feel like a mortal threat.

Lester is implying that the conflict in churches arises because when church leaders try to change a congregation, especially a dysfunctional one, the church's biological sense of survival instinct kicks in. In fact, dysfunctional churches could be said to be churches on hyper-survival alert, because everyone in them feels threatened by everyone else, especially leaders with new ideas. Those good, Christian church members who are saying nasty things about you do so because they feel threatened by you. Some sort of ideal of theirs, even if it is an irrational, problematic ideal, is threatened. *They don't feel safe!* Lester says this about such behavior:

> There is, essentially, one reason why people generate these kinds of behaviors—defensive reactions. These responses do not produce troublesome and unpleasant behaviors by accident. Rather they are designed to make people act badly. They are supposed to turn people into a problem. In addition, the degree to which someone's behavior is a problem is directly proportional to the strength of their defensive reaction. The more intense the defensive reaction, the more problematic the behaviors. The more frequent the defensive reactions, the more frequently the difficult behaviors will occur.
>
> Why are defensive reactions designed this way? Because the whole purpose is to make trouble, to be destructive, disabling, dangerous and fearsome.[6]

Conflict over worship arises when people feel threatened. Worship is a very personal event for those committed to it. Changing worship can feel threatening for those who find deep meaning in particular forms and elements of worship. This feeling of threat is magnified among those who are elderly and already facing great loss in their lives. Transforming worship can cause a visceral, survival reaction to change. People don't resist because they are ignorant, rigid, or selfish. They resist because they feel as though they are losing everything, especially that foundational experience of worship that helps them deal with all the other losses.

At Calvin Presbyterian, those of us leading the changes in worship have had our share of nasty comments from folks who have not liked our change. As I have often told people, being criticized in the midst of change is just part of the price we pay for leading a church. Our task is to determine how threatening their criticism is. Does it represent the tip of an iceberg with deep danger lurking underneath, or does it represent an isolated, free-floating chip of ice. What the people represent is hard to gauge, but typically, when faced with criticism, I spend a lot of time talking to others to gain a sense of how pervasive the feelings are. If they are pervasive and the criticism is the tip of an iceberg, I start to change what I am changing. In other words, I may advocate pulling back, I may advocate discontinuing a new venture, or I may advocate modifying what we are doing.

Too often what magnifies the conflict is the extent to which pastors and worship leaders feel threatened by members' reactions to change. The members may react in a way that isn't particularly Christian (perhaps after hinting at their discomfort for a time before that—hints that the worship leaders or the pastor barely picked up), and that evokes defensiveness among leaders. So leaders respond in ways that may be Christianlike on the outside but defensive and survival-oriented on the inside. Pastors may offer well-articulated sermons critical of those who disagree with them. Or they may push back with their authority, suggesting that because they have gone to seminary and are ordained, they know what is best. This defensive pushback doesn't help the situation; it increases members' defensiveness. And so the church gets caught in a spiraling cycle of defensive responses that escalates.

The task in transforming worship is to lead people by helping them feel safe. Transformation is a scary thing. Whether the change involves major life transitions—going to college, starting a new job, getting married, changing our diet, or engaging in a prayer discipline—or normal ones such as birthdays, the time of transformation is always difficult. We are unsure of what we are doing. We are unsure of the outcome. We know we can't go back, but we are scared of what may come. We feel like we are standing on shaky ground. And we have a heightened sense of vigilance, carefully checking every small blip to see if it is threatening or not. Whenever we go through a normal life transformation, we are often surrounded by people who help us feel safe—resident assistants and staff at college, family and friends at the wedding, nutritional guides with a new diet, and prayer partners or spiritual directors with a new prayer discipline. Our role as leaders of a church undergoing transformation is to help people feel safe and hopeful so that the change doesn't evoke survival defensiveness. Never underestimate the power of defensiveness in people, and always assume that resistance arises out of conceptual survival instinct.

If we are to lead a church through worship transformation, we need to adopt strategies that overcome defensiveness and resistance. In the following section, we will look at four strategies for transforming a congregation's worship. This transformation is based on a principle that underlies much of this book—that any transformation and change must be rooted in God's calling for the church. A church has to base worship on what God is calling them to do, not on what a leader wants to do, or on the fears a congregation has over what they may have to do. But even God-directed transformations evoke defensiveness.

Strategy 1: Make the Transition Gradually

As I have already said, over the years I have consistently noticed that one problem above all others creates conflict in congregations: church leaders, especially pastors, leading a church too quickly through change. This problem arises most forcefully in regard to worship, but it can be a problem for other areas of the church, too.

Time and again, I have served as a spiritual director for pastors who are embroiled in conflict because they led the church through transformation, only to have church members push back in a particularly spiteful and painful way. Often the push-back is started by a small cadre of members, complaining about this or that change. Then the movement grows. The pastor faces a dangerous moment. Give in to their demands too easily and the members, sensing his weakness, eat him for dinner. Be too stubborn, and they try to break her apart by becoming especially malicious, accusing the pastor of all sorts of seemingly bizarre behaviors. These members' behavior becomes dramatically un-Christian. Either way, they create a situation in which the pastor has to decide: Do I abdicate? Do I fight back? Do I give in? What do I do?

Certainly pastors, leaders, and members are called to live up to the guidance Paul gives the church for how we are to treat one another: "Be of the same mind, having the same love, being in full accord and of one mind. Do nothing from selfish ambition or conceit, but in humility regard others as better than yourselves. Let each of you look not to your own interests, but to the interests of others. Let the same mind be in you that was in Christ Jesus" (Phil. 2:2–5). Despite this calling, the reality is that when people feel threatened, they look much more to biology than to Paul. The question among pastoral leaders hurt by members often is, "How could they have treated me this way? They are supposed to be Christians." The answer often lies in the fact that the pastors pushed the members too hard and evoked their defensiveness.

What many pastoral leaders don't realize is that even good Christians misbehave when they feel run over. Here is the gist of the problem: Often pastoral leaders come to a congregation, especially in denominations where pastors are called by a church (as opposed to those "sent" by a bishop), and are told by the lay leaders that the church wants to change. These pastoral leaders take them at their word, so when they come to the church, they go about making changes. The problem is that what seems like a *minor* step for a pastor who is full of new ideas, spawned by years of study and training, may be a *major* step for church members who do not have the same background.

When pastors graduate from seminary, often they leave with so many great ideas of what can be done to resurrect churches. They then go to seminars that fill them with ideas of how to transform a church. I have even led many of these seminars, and I have filled many a pastor with wonderful ideas on how to transform their congregations. And I am sure that many have followed my advice and have gotten into trouble, because they just went too fast for their congregations. The ideas pastors bring to a congregation may not be wrong, but the pace at which we bring them may be. What seems like one small step for us may seem like one giant leap for others.

We forget that the members only know what they have experienced, and they are largely ignorant of the great changes taking place in other churches around the country. Even if what they have experienced hasn't worked, they have not had the opportunity to scan the landscape and to understand what does or doesn't work. And what limited exposure they may have had to different ways of doing things may have made them feel alienated.

I have a rule that I follow and advocate when making changes. It can be summed up in three change formulas:

1. Make the change small and early in the fall.
2. If waiting till fall is a bummer, make it in the summer.
3. If waiting becomes agony, change it after Epiphany.

I am pretty disciplined in following this guidance. I rarely allow any significant changes in worship after early September. Typically, the best time to make adjustments is when school begins, because that is the point at which parents and even grandparents are most flexible. They are already adapting to changes. Plus, often these folks have been spotty in attending church during the summer, so they don't always know if the changes are recent or were done awhile ago. Because they are more adaptable, their defensive instincts are lessened.

When pastors make changes in the fall, they should also make them small. Now, smallness is subjective. For Calvin Presbyterian, because we have made so many changes over time, our changes can be significantly larger than in churches that have made no changes for a long time. But when I first started here, our changes were very small. The first change I encouraged in worship was offering silent prayer and a Taizé-like response to our prayer of confession, which we introduced in September. Prior to this, we said a printed prayer of confession together, and then the pastor immediately offered an assurance of pardon. Because I have always believed in the power of silence in worship,

I advocated following the printed prayer with a thirty-second period of silence for personal confessions. Then this was followed by one verse of a chant, something such as, "O Lord, hear my prayer; O Lord, hear my prayer. When I call, answer me. O Lord, hear my prayer; O Lord, hear my prayer. Come and listen to me."[7] We change the response each month and tie the song thematically to the season.

This was a simple change for me, but for members of the church it was fairly substantial. For the rest of the year, our worship leaders changed nothing until the following fall. Then we decided to offer more contemporary music. We did this by having the choir sing a more contemporary anthem twice a month. Periodically, we would use a more contemporary middle hymn, printed on a bulletin insert. The congregation did this for a year. During that year, a task force created a new songbook filled with both contemporary songs as well as some cherished songs that had been left out of *The Presbyterian Hymnal*. That songbook was introduced during the following fall, and we told the congregation that we would choose hymns from it periodically, and that they would always be the middle hymns in our services. One thing I have learned is that if you introduce a new song in the middle of worship, people will forgive you, but not if you do so with the first or last hymn. People who resist change remember what hits them either first or last. It's the middle they forget about. The following year we made a decision to have the last hymn always be contemporary, the first one always be traditional, and the middle always be one that fits best with the Scripture and sermon. As you can see, we made changes in the fall; each one was relatively small, and over time we created large-scale cumulative changes.

This last point brings out an issue that I think is crucial for churches. Too often pastors new to a congregation are in a hurry for change. Perhaps they want to make changes quickly because they don't expect to be there long, and they feel the need to build up a set of accomplishments they can tout in interviews with new churches. Perhaps they can't stand something in their new church, and they want to make the changes quickly to make themselves more comfortable. Perhaps their hurry rises out of a need to be deemed a success, and because of the growth they hope will occur from these changes. Perhaps they have large egos and think they just know what is right and that everyone else is ignorant. The reasons are many, but the result is the same: their hurry makes members scurry.

I have another principle that I have maintained since I came to Calvin Presbyterian Church: *If I lead as though I'm going to retire from this church, then I have all the time in the world.* When pastors lead from this perspective, it allows us to go slow and take a long-term view of building relationships, not accomplishments.

The other caveats, making changes in the summer or after Epiphany, are extensions of making changes small and in the fall. There are times when, for a variety of reasons, churches just can't wait until the fall. A few years ago the worship leaders at Calvin Church made a somewhat significant change at the beginning of summer because we wanted to see what kind of reaction we would get from the congregation, and we thought summer was a time when people might be more amenable to the changes we were proposing. Each year the music staff visits other churches in the area that we sense we could learn from. We visited an emergent congregation in Pittsburgh and thought two things they did would work in our worship. The first was that they started worship with a gathering song that was always contemporary and energetic. Our service usually started with announcements followed by a traditional hymn. Also, at the end of the service, this church had everyone gather in a circle, hold hands, and sing the doxology. We didn't think congregants at Calvin could gather in a circle because of the configuration of the sanctuary, but we did think that it might make the service seem a bit more intimate if it closed with members holding hands in the pews while a pastor offered a prayer of benediction. By doing this during the summer, when many people were traveling for vacation and weren't as focused on what the congregation was doing in worship, we were able to institute the change during a low-resistance time.

Only as a last resort will I ever allow a change between fall and summer, and if we must make a change, we wait until after Epiphany. The reason is that after the Christmas season, people have been through so many activities, often the sanctuaries have been decorated so much, and we have done so many different kinds of worship services through Advent and Christmas that the appearance of something new is not as jarring.

The point of all this is to reduce defensiveness among members and to actually build trust during transition and transformation. When change is gradual, and people sense that leaders are acting slowly and with sensitivity to them, they are more likely to support change. As a last rule of thumb: if you get strong resistance to what you do, back off, simplify, and make the steps smaller and slower. Just by doing this, you will build and restore trust.

Strategy 2: Integrate Ideas from All Corners

Another problem many churches face when transforming worship is that they tend to go only with what one generation wants rather than what many generations may want. In our modern worship wars, the tendency has been to discount the older generations in the rush to appeal to younger generations, or to ignore the desires of younger generations in order to appease the older generations who have financial clout. Either way, the focus is not on multigenerational worship but on uni-generational worship. To create multigenerational worship means paying attention to what all generations have to say and then finding ways to integrate their ideas.

At Calvin Presbyterian Church this means that before we consider changes, we try to talk the changes through from all perspectives. A significant change suggested by our staff will go through our worship and arts committee. That committee may form a task force composed of members from different generations who will then come back to the committee, or it may deal with the change just as a committee. Along the way, the committee and staff will informally solicit the opinions of a variety of members. By the time a final decision is made, committee members and staff may have spoken formally or informally to forty or fifty people.

For instance, to put together our songbook, we formed a committee that represented every age group. The committee had a teen representative (who now has gone on to a music career, including a stint as music director of an urban emergent church), one in her twenties, one in her thirties, one in his early forties, and one in his mid-fifties who was an advocate of traditional worship. The majority of songs selected for the songbook were contemporary, but the committee also added standards that had been left out of *The Presbyterian Hymnal*, such as "Rock of Ages," "I Surrender All," "In the Garden," and "I Wonder as I Wander." We solicited input from all ages and tried to be sensitive to them all, even though our focus was creating a contemporary songbook.

The worship leaders take this same approach, as much as they can, when listening to complaints. When moving a congregation's worship forward, few are shy about offering their complaints and criticisms, but how pastors and other leaders respond makes a big difference. Often we try to respond to complaints in what I would call an *asymmetrical* way. What that means is that just because a person complains about something in a particular way doesn't mean we have to address it in a like-mannered way. For instance, I spoke earlier about several complaints about how noisy the beginning of our worship service was. A *symmetrical* way of dealing with it would have been to put up signs outside the sanctuary asking people to be quiet upon entering the sanctuary, or having someone stand up three minutes before the service, asking people to pray in reverent silence. Both approaches might have been effective, but they also would have caused us to seem unfriendly and stodgy to visitors and younger people, who like to talk. The asymmetrical way leaders at Calvin dealt with this issue was to combine those complaints with my concerns about the call to worship and how ineffective it was. It led us to create the new way to start worship discussed earlier—which we introduced in the fall. The asymmetry was that we responded to the complaints with something new that took care of several issues. We didn't take care of the issue by addressing it head on but by creating a new approach. This kind of asymmetry requires the creativity to look for alternatives rather than the apparent but symmetrical answers, such as doing nothing or doing what the complainer wants, both of which can create more problems.

Strategy 3: Know When to Do Battle and When to Give Up

Knowing when to do battle and when to give up may be the hardest wisdom of all to learn. The fact is that moving a congregation forward is often a matter of balancing what can be achieved with what can be achieved only at the high price of division. Too many pastors go down in flames in their churches because they do battle in a losing cause. I don't like the metaphor of transforming worship as a battle, but in some cases the term is apt.

Just as I don't like calling the transformation of worship a battle, I am also not entirely comfortable with consulting the ancient Chinese military warrior-philosopher Sun Tzu on strategies for transforming worship. Still, he offers wisdom to us in the present, insights culled from ancient military campaigns. This wisdom can guide us in helping our congregations become more open to the Holy. In his two-thousand-year-old classic, *The Art of War*, Sun Tzu talks about how to do battle effectively. He says, "When you do battle, even if you are winning, if you continue for a long time it will dull your forces and blunt your edge; if you besiege a citadel, your strength will be exhausted. If you keep your armies out in the field for a long time, your supplies will be insufficient."[8]

What does this have to do with transitions in worship? What he is saying, as it applies to worship, is that even if we leaders are getting our way, the cost of constantly fighting members will cause us to lose in the long run, because it will sap our spirit, our energy, and our effectiveness. I think he would say that if our efforts are taking too long, if we are fighting an entrenched opposition, or if we are working too hard to get allies to our cause, we will lose in the long run. Our efforts will fail by dividing the church and will lead to slow attrition, even if we are gaining new members.

Knowing when to push on toward transformation, and when to give up, is key. And there are three keys to dealing with transitional conflict. First, we need to recognize that sometimes even the best ideas will not work because they will lead to defensiveness in others. Some dysfunctional congregations are so used to failure that they almost instinctively resist change no matter what, and our attempts to push for change will fail, especially if we have not taken the time to instill trust between them and us. Sometimes building this trust can take years, which can be very frustrating for pastors and other leaders with lots of ideas. If we face resistance but keep persisting to the point at which we are becoming defensive as leaders, we have already lost the fight. Our persistence, and the backlash it evokes, creates the conditions for a long-running division that may last long after we, burned-out over our battles, have left the church.

Not all conflict is bad, for all transformations involve conflict, but conflict that leads to fighting, fleeing, or freezing is tragic in a church. It is better, when faced with one or all of those sensations, to pull back. So the first key to dealing with transitional conflict is that *change should proceed only when a relatively high level of trust and support exists between leaders and members, especially those who aren't leaders.*

A second key to dealing with conflict is recognizing that *whenever leaders proceed in the face of opposition, they have to do so both gently and firmly.* Sometimes it becomes apparent that making a change is absolutely crucial to a church's future, despite resistance. I have faced that at Calvin Church. When I came to the church, the sanctuary and much of the church was in poor physical condition. Among other problems, the lighting in the sanctuary was dark, the carpet was wrinkled and a potential tripping hazard, and the choir sat on old, wooden folding chairs that didn't seem safe. I knew that we had to renovate the sanctuary, which meant embarking on a capital campaign. I think most members were behind the changes, but I also know that some were not, and they let me know it.

I felt I had no choice but to lead the church in that direction. First, I sensed that it was God's calling for us, and I had prayed a lot over that even before coming to the church as its pastor. Second, I thought that some parts of the sanctuary were outright dangerous, especially the wrinkled carpet that could trip people with a poor sense of balance. Third, I believed that we could not grow without the renovations. The lighting was so dark, the aesthetics so bland, and the chancel area so cramped that it had little appeal to visitors. So I proceeded in leading the congregation forward, but I did so both gently and firmly.

The issue that arises when leaders proceed in the face of resistance is that we will be criticized, yet we need to know how to respond in a positive way. Thus, when someone complains or is critical, we *must* validate what that person says, even if it feels threatening or hurtful to us. This is what it means to be gentle and firm. We keep moving ahead, but we do so in a caring way. For example, as Calvin Church proceeded to deal with the problems of our sanctuary, one member said to me that he felt we were wasting money on renovating the whole sanctuary when we could just put in new carpeting and save ourselves $100,000. I agreed with him. In essence I said, "I hear you. I don't want to do this renovation at all. I hate asking for money. And I worry that a lot of people like you will be upset by it. But at the same time, I also know that if we don't do all of this now, we're going to have to do it piecemeal over the next ten years, and I don't have the energy for that. We'd start with replacing the carpeting. Then we'd replace the choir chairs. Then we'd have to repaint the sanctuary. Then we'd have to add new lighting to replace the old lighting. And if we grow, we'd have to keep making changes. I don't have the energy to go to the congregation every two years asking for money. And I certainly don't have the energy to ask you." (I laughed as I said it.) The point is that I was trying to be gentle with him by validating his concerns and letting him know I shared them. But at the same time, I was firm that I thought this was the prudent course. I kept talking with him over the years, and he stayed in the congregation. He is now a big supporter of the changes we have made. The firmness told him that we were moving forward with or without him, but the gentleness said that we cared about his concerns.

Finally, sometimes churches make changes that can feel as though they follow God's calling, but it becomes apparent that they just won't work. So, when these events happen, a third key to dealing with transitional conflict is recognizing that *when change isn't working, we may have to go back to the way things were and authentically make a big deal about how we leaders have heard the congregation and agree with them.* Doing so can restore and instill a level of trust that is golden. We have had numerous situations at Calvin Church in which we tried new things and then cut the experiments off early. When we did so, we actually enhanced trust.

An example of cutting off an experiment and thus restoring trust came after Calvin Church's attempt to offer a contemporary worship service. This was the late 1990s, and we weren't sure if we were called to do contemporary worship, so we did a test. We decided that for ten months we would offer contemporary worship once a month. The church has a lot of musical talent, so this was not a hard thing for us to do. Bruce Smith, our music director, is a jazz and rock pianist who grew up with Christian contemporary music. Our keyboard accompanist, DeWayne Segafredo, does lighting and sound for some of the biggest and most popular musical acts in Western Pennsylvania every weekend. We had access to both expertise and equipment. Our associate music director, Toni Schlemmer, had a background in drama and understood the aesthetics. And so we embarked on our contemporary experiment.

The services were done well, and some members—perhaps 20 percent—loved it. Another 40 percent had little opinion one way or another. They could worship in either contemporary or traditional services. But a strong 40 percent absolutely hated it. Just the sight of drums ruined worship for them. Each month they let leaders know, and they began complaining loudly to the 40 percent who had originally been ambivalent about contemporary worship. The voices of dissent were growing. Still, we had told the congregation that this was a ten-month experiment. Our thought was, "It's only once-a-month, so what's the big deal?"

After three months of this experiment we concluded that not only was there a lot of discontent in the congregation but also that the worship staff wasn't even sure we liked contemporary worship. We had the talent, but we didn't have the passion. And we were tired of the complaining. So we cut the experiment off after only three months. We told the congregation in January that we knew contemporary wasn't right for us. Sometimes you hear God best in what doesn't work. Failure is discernment, too. So we told them that we were cutting off the experiment early. We also told them that we appreciated their willingness to experiment and that their willingness said a lot about their spiritual maturity. This was and is a true statement. We finally told them that this experiment really helped us understand our music program better and that we were thankful for the opportunity.

Some of our members were disappointed, but ending the experiment early also told the congregation that we valued their opinions and that we weren't there to just run all over them in the service of our vision. Cutting the experiment early reestablished the congregation's trust, especially among those who felt steamrolled by our experiment.

Strategy 4: Explain Change and Transformation

I believe that the need to explain change and transformation to a congregation before launching it is something of a no-brainer, but that doesn't mean that we pastors are good at it. Too often changes in churches are introduced with little or no explanation. Just as a field needs to be fertilized and plowed before planting, the ground for transformation needs to be fertilized and plowed before change is instilled.

What does it mean to explain change? It doesn't mean just explaining the practical changes in worship on the day those changes are made. It means communicating early and often the modifications that are taking place, the thinking behind them, when they will happen, and what the hoped for outcome will be. At Calvin we try to communicate the need for change and transformation in a variety of ways. First, I often preach on the need for transformation and change on both a personal and a congregational level. Over the years, the congregation has heard me say that a person who is not growing spiritually is dying spiritually, and the congregation that is not growing spiritually is dying spiritually. Spiritual change doesn't take place only on the inside. It is manifested on the outside. A person growing in prayer will pray more often, and she will change her life as a result. A church that is growing spiritually will seek God's guidance more often and will change what it does as a result. I preach transformation, and I will often talk about our church's past transformations and the graces they have wrought.

For instance, I have preached about the renovation to our sanctuary eleven years ago, speaking about the positive impact it has had on our congregation in enhancing worship. I have preached about our failures, and the failures of our contemporary worship in particular. I have talked about how we put together our songbook and how important this was to the life of the congregation. I have spoken often about how the mission of our older members should be to our younger members, and how the mission of our younger members should be to our older members. I have explained our theory of multigenerational worship and how it requires openness to transformation. I also write about similar themes on occasion in our newsletter. In doing this, I am fertilizing the field for future planting.

When Calvin Church engages in changes, all the aspects of the modifications to the congregation are explained in our newsletter, in our bulletin, and verbally. In communicating each change, those of us leading the initiative try our best to communicate the *specifics* of the change, the *why* of the change, the *hope* of the change, the *process* of the change, and our *sensitivity* in doing the change. We will ask the congregation to bear with us, and we will tell them that the purpose is always to enhance worship. For example, as I write this book, the front of our sanctuary is being changed to enhance the sound. The instruments are being moved around so that instead of having the choir sit at the center of our chancel, between our baby grand piano on the left side and our other keyboards, guitar, and drums on the right, we will cluster the musicians together around the piano. The problem is that this change will create a lopsided look. The choir, which had been centered in the chancel, will be off-center, so that their right flank starts at the center and then extends to the left side and onto a platform. Meanwhile, the musicians will be clustered just a bit right of center and extending to the right side of the chancel. These alterations create a look that's a bit askew for a sanctuary where the choir has been centered for more than a century. The lack of symmetry will be a problem for some.

Recognizing that the change may cause problems for some, our worship leaders and staff first explained the *specifics* of the change. We told the congregation exactly what we were doing, with an emphasis on how the decision came about. We placed a short article in our newsletter for the month as well as one in our Sunday bulletin for several weeks. We instituted the change on September 6 (a moderately "small and in the fall" change). We also made a verbal announcement about the change in worship that Sunday and the previous two Sundays. The articles specifically talked about what we have done. In the verbal announcement, we showed people what we had done. And we told them how this idea first came about from the music staff, then through the worship and arts committee, and then was approved by the session.

Next, we talked in detail about the *why* of change. In this case, we told them that despite the lopsided look, the change would enhance the sound of worship by doing two things: first, by placing our choir in the geographical, if not the apparent, front center of the sanctuary; and, second, clustering the musicians together so that they can communicate with one another. The first comment requires explanation so that you understand what it meant. As part of our renovation in 1998, we added an enclosed wing to the left of the sanctuary that juts out into our fellowship hall, adding fifty seats to the side of the sanctuary. The chancel of the sanctuary had been at the geographical front and center of the unrenovated sanctuary, but after we added the wing, the center was farther to the left, while the chancel was geographically farther to the right. Moving the choir onto the platform where the instruments had been put them in the geographical center, even though it looks as though they are left of center. We explained to the congregation that the previous configuration with the choir under an arch at the center, muted their sound to a certain extent. By moving them out from under the arch and to the left, we were enhancing sound by placing them in the true center of the front of the church and by bringing them out from under the arch. At the same time, we were also allowing the musicians to communicate with one another by clustering them, which enhanced the music.

This leads to the next thing we communicated: the *hope of change*. We emphasized that the changes are *for the congregation*, and our hope was that it would enhance their worship experience. We acknowledged that the look would be awkward, but our hope was that this would be compensated by their enhanced ability to hear the nuances of our music.

Next, we talked about the *process* of change. For the most part, this meant telling them when the change would take place and how it would be done. We told them what to expect and when to expect it. The process of this particular change was fairly straightforward, but in changes that occur in phases, we want to make sure the congregation understands each change.

Finally, we talked about our being *sensitive* to the congregation's perceptions about the change. We thanked them sincerely and honestly for their allowing us to experiment and to try new things to enhance worship at Calvin Church. We praised then sincerely for their sensitivity to us. And we told them that we do want their feedback on both the look and the sound, but feedback with an understanding of what we are trying to do. This is not fake praise and sensitivity. It is honest and heartfelt. All the members of our worship staff deeply appreciate the freedom to be creative that the congregation gives us, and we let them know that we appreciate them creating an environment in which we can experiment.

The whole point is that if churches are to transform worship so that people can experience and encounter the Holy in worship, church leaders have to communicate more than just the facts of the change. When people understand the reason for transformation and are appreciated for their willingness to be adaptive, they are more likely to go along with changes.

Final Thoughts

Ultimately, transformation is hard for a congregation. No congregation, unless it is one that split away from another with the expectation of making sweeping changes, embraces transformation wholeheartedly. None of us embraces it wholeheartedly. I have certainly gone through a lot of changes over the years, and I have not appreciated all of them. But I have recognized the need for them.

Transformation is difficult precisely because it is fraught with uncertainty. Will this transformation lead to something better? Will it cause pain? Will it take away what is good and leave only something bad in its wake? What will happen to us? Will it lead to success or failure? There are no guarantees.

Still, when churches take the practical steps necessary for healthy transformation, they give it every opportunity to succeed. When church leaders are sensitive to how threatening change is to people, when we validate and assuage their fears, we help them overcome resistance. When leaders are patient with the process of transformation, we give the congregation room to grow at a pace that helps it integrate the changes in a healthy way. When leaders are sensitive to the concerns of all worshipers, and integrate their ideas into the changes, everyone becomes part of the process. By only doing battle when necessary, and being willing to give up when necessary, we create meaningful change while simultaneously building trust. When we do our work explaining change, we set up the conditions for healthy transformation to take root and grow.

For us to hear God's calling in transforming a church's worship is not enough. A clear picture of what needs to change to bring all generations to an experience of God in worship is not enough. We also need to do the practical things that allow transformation to work. Employing the steps offered in this chapter will go a long way toward making positive transitions.

Reflection Questions

1. As you reflect on the whole chapter, what concepts or points stood out for you and why?
2. As you think about leading your church to make changes in worship that would enhance the encounter with the Holy, what are the obstacles?

3. What are the conflict points that arise in your church when contemplating changes to the worship service?
4. Discuss specific strategies and tactics you could employ to help the church transform its worship in a way that is less threatening to members.

Notes

Introduction

1. Diana Butler Bass, *The Practicing Congregation: Imagining a New Old Church* (Herndon, VA: Alban Institute, 2004), 80.

Chapter 1: Where's the Holy

1. George G. Hunter III, *The Celtic Way of Evangelism: How Christianity Can Reach the West . . . Again* (Nashville: Abingdon Press, 2000), 13–35.
2. Ibid., 37.
3. N. Graham Standish, *Becoming a Blessed Church* (Herndon, VA: Alban Institute, 2005), ch. 2.
4. Diana Butler Bass, *The Practicing Congregation: Imagining a New Old Church* (Herndon, VA: Alban Institute, 2004),18–19, 81–90.
5. Dan Kimball, *Emerging Worship: Creating New Worship Gatherings for New Generations* (Grand Rapids: Zondervan, 2004), 44–45.
6. Ibid., 5.
7. Lillian Kwon, "Largest Christian Groups Report Membership Decline," *The Christian Post*, February 25, 2009, www.christianpost.com/article/20090225/largest-christian-groups-report-membership-decline/index.html (accessed 2/11/10).
8. Kimball, *Emerging Worship*, 80.
9. David Hackett Fischer, *Albion's Seed: Four British Folkways in America* (Oxford, UK: Oxford University Press, 1989), 121.
10. Ibid., 122.
11. Eric Reed, "Return to Ritual," ChristianityToday.com, March 13, 2009, http://www.christiantoday.com/le/preachingworship/worship/returntoritual.htm (accessed 2/11/2010).

Chapter 2: Tradition or Culture—Which One?

1. Adrian van Kaam, *Formative Spirituality*, vol. 1, *Fundamental Formation* (New York: Crossroads Publishing, 1989), 301.
2. Ibid., 95.
3. Diana Butler Bass, *The Practicing Congregation: Imagining a New Old Church* (Herndon, VA: Alban Institute, 2004), 80.
4. Thomas Kelly, *A Testament of Devotion* (San Francisco: HarperSanFrancisco, 1992), pg. 3.

5. Van Kaam, *Formative Spirituality*, 262. Van Kaam uses his own set of terms for the states of mind we know as the conscious, preconscious, shared consciousness, and the unconscious. They are the *focal, pre-, inter-, infra-consciousness,* and *transconsciousness.* For the sake of understanding them better in this discussion, I have used the more familiar terms rather than van Kaam's, with the exception of maintaining his term *transconscious.*

6. Ibid., 263.

7. Eric Elnes, "Practicing Worship: From Message to Incarnation," in *From Nomads to Pilgrims: Stories from Practicing Congregations,* ed. Diana Butler Bass and Joseph Stewart-Sicking (Herndon, VA: Alban Institute, 2006), 72.

Chapter 3: What Are We Trying to Do?

1. Urban T. Holmes, *A History of Christian Spirituality: An Analytical Introduction* (San Francisco: Harper & Row, 1980), 3–5.

2. C. S. Lewis, *Mere Christianity* (New York: HarperOne, 2000), 196–97.

3. Ibid., 199.

4. Reproduced from *Book of Common Worship,* p. 17. Copyright (c) 1993 Westminster John Knox Press. Used by permission of Westminster John Knox Press.

5. Martin Luther (1529), "A Mighty Fortress," trans. Frederick H. Hedge (1852), http://www.hymnsite.com/lyrics/umh110.sht (accessed January 10, 2010).

6. "Be Thou My Vision," Irish 8th–10th cen., trans. Mary E. Byrne (1880–1931); http://www.musicanet.org/robokopp/eire/bethoumy.htm (accessed January 10, 2010).

7. John Newton (1705–1807), "Amazing Grace," http://www.constitution.org/col/amazing_grace.htm (accessed January 10, 2010).

Chapter 4: Understanding Our Era

1. Ken Wilber, *The Marriage of Sense and Soul: Integrating Science and Religion* (New York: Random House, 1998).

2. Ibid., 12.

3. Ibid.

4. John Maynard Keynes, *General Theory of Employment* (London, Macmillan Cambridge Univ. Press for Royal Economic Society, 1936), 6:383.

5. Wilber, 120–21.

6. Walter Isaacson, *Einstein: His Life and Universe* (New York: Simon & Schuster, 2007), 94.

7. Leonard Sweet, *Aquachurch: Essential Leadership Arts for Piloting Your Church in Today's Fluid Culture* (Loveland, CO: Group, 1999), 19.

8. Ibid., 54–55.

9. Ibid., 35–36.

10. Ibid., 71–74.

11. "Frederick J. Eikerenkoetter II: 'Reverend Ike' Pioneered Televangelism," Chicago Sun-Times online, July 31, 2009.

CHAPTER 5: INTEGRATED WORSHIP

1. Thomas Kelly, 3.
2. Ibid., 9.

CHAPTER 6: LEADING A CHURCH TOWARD HOLY WORSHIP

1. William Strauss and Neil Howe, *Generations: The History of America's Future, 1584 to 2069* (New York: William Morrow, 1991), 299.
2. Ibid., 299–304.
3. Gregory W. Lester, *Power with People: How to Handle Just about Anyone to Accomplish Just about Anything* (Houston: Ashcroft Press, 1995), 8.
4. Ibid., 27.
5. Ibid., 34–35.
6. Ibid., 50.
7. "O Lord Hear My Prayer," *Songs and Prayers from Taizé* (Chicago: GIA Publications, 1991), no. 20.
8. Sun Tzu, *The Art of War,* trans. Thomas Cleary (Boston: Shambhala, 1991), 11.

264
S7856

LINCOLN CHRISTIAN UNIVERSITY

122060

3 4711 00201 4498